S0-AAD-375

CONTENTS

CONTENTS

A quarterly journal that serves as a repository for the very best of African American preaching and provides practical and creative resources for persons in ministry.

VOLUME 9, NUMBER 4 / FALL 2006 (ISSN 1094-0111)

Chief Executive Officer of Hope for Life International, Inc. Frank A. Thomas

President and Publisher Martha Simmons

Coexecutive Editors Katara A. Washington and Eugene L. Gibson Jr.

Advisory Board Members James Abbington, Brad R. Braxton, Claudette A. Copeland, Marcus D. Cosby, Cynthia L. Hale, Donald Hilliard Jr., Alison P. Gise Johnson, Rudolph W. McKissick Jr., Otis Moss III, Jasmin W. Sculark, Robert Smith Jr., Gardner C. Taylor, Ralph Douglas West, and Jeremiah A. Wright Jr.

Project Manager Victoria McGoey

Advertising Manager Charlesetta Gipson

Copyeditor Rebecca Irwin-Diehl

Theological and other opinions expressed by the editors and contributors are not necessarily those of Hope for Life International, Inc. or the publisher. Unsolicited manuscripts that are received and considered for publication must be original unpublished works. Please see our submissions guidelines at www.TheAfricanAmericanPulpit.com or call 412-364-1688 for further information. Please mail submissions to: *The African American Pulpit,* P.O. Box 15347, Pittsburgh, PA 15237.

INDIVIDUAL SUBSCRIPTION RATES: $40.00 per year. Library subscription rates: $59.00 per year. Subscribers outside the United States, please remit in U.S. funds. Subscribers in Canada and other subscribers outside the United States, please add $7.50 per year for additional postage. Single copies are also available. Seminarians receive a special discounted rate; call for information. All prices are subject to change. Subscription orders should be sent to The African American Pulpit, P.O. Box 381587, Germantown, TN 38183 or call 800-509-TAAP.

ADVERTISERS: For information, please address queries to Advertising Manager, *The African American Pulpit,* 1825 Riverdale Road, Germantown, TN 38138 or call 901-526-3364. The publication of advertising in *The African American Pulpit* does not constitute endorsement by Hope for Life International, Inc., *The African American Pulpit,* its publisher, its editors, or its advisory board members. Advertisers and their agencies assume liability for all content of advertisements printed or representations made therein.

BACK ISSUES: Dynamic and exciting back issues of *The African American Pulpit* are available, **and many are on sale!** Please contact Customer Service at 800-509-8227 or www.TheAfricanAmericanPulpit.com.

POSTMASTER: Send subscription questions and address changes to: Customer Service, The African American Pulpit, P.O. Box 381587, Germantown, TN 38183, or call 800-509-8227.

Visit our website: www.TheAfricanAmericanPulpit.com   Back Issues On Sale!   **3**

SALUTING
Seminarians

Katara A. Washington and
Eugene L. Gibson Jr.

To be or Not to be in Seminary—is that still the question?

This question raises others: In a world of TV ministry and "mega" and now "giga" churches, are people grappling with going to institutions of higher learning where they might spend time in preparation with God? In a culture where the gospel has seemingly been laced with Americanized capitalism that has traded the Cross for cash, cameras, and crowds, are there any men and women standing like Jacob at the Jabbok wrestling against God, man, and self? *The African American Pulpit* is excited to answer such questions with a resounding YES! Not only are there many outstanding seminary students who are striving and struggling, but we have the pleasure of sharing some of their ministry with you in this Fall 2006 Seminarians' Issue.

We had a really tough time choosing our three winners in our third seminarians contest. We did finally settle on three outstanding sermons to award monetarily and to print in this issue. However, we just couldn't stop there. We've selected 11 other sermons to share with you. We hope that you will be blessed by the inspiring words and encouraged by the new crop of seminarians working in the vineyard. (None of these persons have been preaching for more than five years.) Thanks to all seminarians who submitted sermons. We were truly blessed by your ministries, and we pray that you will continue to use your preaching gifts to bless, encourage, convict, challenge, and inspire the people of God.

In addition to our powerful seminarian sermons in this issue, we've also included esteemed elders Caesar Clark, Sandy Ray, and Charles Albert Tindley. You're certain to be challenged and encouraged by their words. And we have several informative articles as usual, such as an article on forming dance ministry and an inspiring reminder on preaching to heal listeners.

We hope that you will enjoy this issue and will be encouraged in your ministry. Next quarter we will give you a taste of the best in hip-hop preaching, so stay tuned.

Send us a note to let us know how *TAAP* is helping your ministry or ways we can better serve you. We'll be waiting to hear from you.

Until next time, keep spreading the word.

Katara A. Washington

Eugene Gibson

In Honor of MEDGAR EVERS

GENE CORNELIUS YOUNG

As the 1963 school year was nearing its end, the television news reported about Civil Rights demonstrations taking place in Birmingham, Alabama, with images of school-age children being bitten by vicious police doges and knocked down by high-powered fire hoses. The children did not seem to be afraid as they faced the wrath of Birmingham's Commissioner of Public Safety, Eugene "Bull" Connor. As they were forcibly put into paddy wagons and taken off to jail, they just kept on singing freedom songs.

As a seventh grade student at Lanier High School in Jackson, Mississippi, I did not know what freedom was. I certainly did not want to be a freedom fighter, and I thanked God that I was not in Alabama. Little did I know that the

spirit of the freedom movement was spreading rapidly across the South and that soon Jackson would be ground-zero in the Civil Rights struggle. I also did not know that much of the planning of the Civil Rights work in Mississippi rested on the shoulders of the field secretary of the NAACP, Medgar Wiley Evers.

I was looking forward to playing for the neighborhood little league baseball team and wearing the prized, pinstriped uniform of the Pirates. In the last week of classes, Freedom Riders were arrested at the Jackson Trailways Bus Station and students at Lanier walked out the next day in protest. I joined my other schoolmates as we exited through the front doors of Lanier High School onto the sidewalks of Maple Street. I did not realize it at the time, but I had become a member of the Civil Rights Movement and one of the youngest freedom fighters.

At the age of twelve, I was arrested along with others and spent several days in the unfriendly and very uncomfortable confines of the livestock compounds on the grounds of the Mississippi State Fairgrounds, and upon being freed, I joined others and went to a community mass meeting. The auditorium was filled to capacity, and the audience applauded when it was announced that we had just been released. Many there that night had come to hear and see the legendary actress and singer Lena Horne, comedian/activist Dick Gregory, and Medgar Wiley Evers, the undisputed leader of the Jackson Civil Rights movement. Jerome Smith, a Congress of Racial Equality (CORE) staff member from New Orleans, who had been severely beaten by an angry mob of white people near McComb, Mississippi, told me that if I went up on the stage and exhorted others to join in the demonstrations, he would take me to New York to tell my story!!! I had to stand in a chair to reach the microphone on the podium and I do not recall what I said that evening, but Lena Horne kissed me and Medgar Evers said that he was proud of

Gene Cornelius Young is an educator and human rights activist.

my impromptu performance. I would not get a chance to wear my pinstriped baseball uniform that summer, but Jerome Smith kept his promise and I was going to New York.

On June 12, 1963, I flew on an airplane for the first time, and upon our arrival we went to the Harlem apartment of David Baldwin, the brother of the prolific writer James Baldwin, and when he opened the door, he greeted us with the tragic news that Medgar Evers had been murdered in Jackson. My first airplane flight would be forever linked with the morbid memory of one of Mississippi's greatest native sons making the supreme sacrifice in the struggle for freedom. O for more people like Medgar who will not shrink in the fight for justice. I have always been inspired by the words and deeds of Medgar Wiley Evers (July 2, 1925–June 12, 1963):

"Ladies and Gentlemen, I think it is appropriate at this time that I make a confession to you before I go any further and that is: I love the land of my birth. I do not mean just America as a country, but Mississippi, the state in which I was born. The things I say here tonight will be said to you in the hopes of the future when it will not be the case in Mississippi and America, when we will not have to hang our heads in shame or hold our breath when the name Mississippi is mentioned, fearing the worst. But instead, we will be anticipating the best."[1]   ❖

NOTE

1. This quotation from Medgar Wiley Evers is from the pamphlet "Remembering Medgar Evers…For A New Generation," published by the African American Studies Program at the University of Mississippi, 1988.

TEACHING Black Preaching: Encounter and Re-encounter

DALE P. ANDREWS

Throughout my own education in seminary and graduate studies, I was frequently intrigued by the fascination with black preaching traditions among my peers across cultures. And yet, I was also struck by a very real awkwardness in preaching classes designed either to introduce students to black preaching or to mature them in those

Dale P. Andrews is the Martin Luther King, Jr. Professor of Homiletics and Pastoral Theology at Boston University School of Theology, Boston, Massachusetts.

traditions. My intrigue has not waned in teaching those same courses. The challenges facing such courses are as diverse as those students who enroll, not to mention those students who avoid them altogether. Still, two challenges stand out prominently. On the one hand, many African American students and those students from other predominantly folk traditions struggle with the constraining demands of homiletic methods designed to give structure and direction to their sermons; these methods feel "imposed" on their own already developing techniques extending from apprenticeship church traditions. On the other hand, students from other racial or cultural church traditions feel stymied by the search for familiar methodology within the otherwise foreign artistry of folk preaching developed through those mentoring or apprenticeship traditions. I believe these challenges cry out for attention in the immediate future of our homiletic pedagogy or teaching strategies.

The tasks before us, then, remain twofold. The first task involves ways to cultivate homiletic teaching strategies that will develop methodology for black preaching without disrupting the strengths of these apprenticeship traditions. A second task demands that we develop teaching strategies that formulate methodology for those students wholly unfamiliar with the artistry and rhetorical structures of the preaching event. My interest lies in developing a pedagogical construct of apprenticeship traditions in black preaching that will thoroughly shape sermon preparation, homiletic design or methodology, and the preaching event itself. Most instructive texts in black preaching traditions are developed in classic modernist notions of method, much like the predominant texts in mainstream Western church traditions, which emphasize concrete steps or terms to be reproduced in sermon constructions. The pedagogical enterprise I propose here is complicated by the multiple tasks involved when one's class is comprised of novice and mature preachers in black preaching and other students quite unfamiliar with these preaching traditions altogether. Herein I envision an effort that provides the constructive tools of methodology for those deeply familiar with the apprenticeship preaching experience, as well as one that provides the exploring tools of homiletic culture and artistry of preaching for those unfamiliar with the mentoring or apprenticeship models within the black preaching experience.

Many homiletic courses are designed to introduce students to methodologies that guide exegesis with an eye peering toward sermon construction. Exegesis exercises teach us how to explore a biblical text. Language, literature, history of interpretations, the contexts of the authors and original hearers as well as the context of the exegete and contemporary hearers all conflate in our efforts to move from the text to the sermon. Where you locate yourself in the move to the sermon will of course involve your theology of the Word. That is to say, we are influenced greatly by our understanding of how God works through preaching and in the preaching event itself. Your theology of the Word develops in your preaching praxis. I intend theology of the Word to include multiple, but reflexive, meanings. Theology of the Word for preaching certainly includes an understanding of God's revelation through Scripture. The authority of our preaching reflects the authority of Scripture in our church traditions. However, part of the reflexive meanings in the theology of the Word is experiential.

Scripture gives witness to Christ himself as the Word of God. Through the activity of the Holy Spirit, we explore the Word in Scripture and encounter the Word in Christ. Preaching becomes the Word of God as the Holy Spirit reveals God in the exploration and encounter—transforming the limitations or exploration of our words into an encounter with the living Word of God. Others have argued that the Word of God is located in the communication between Scripture and the Church, "a spoken-heard phenomenon."[1] The tasks of biblical interpretation and sermon construction involve the preacher's "spoken-heard" encounter in sermon preparation and the "spoken-heard" re-encounter in preaching the sermon. The re-encounter involves the Word, the preacher, and the hearers in the preaching event.

The starting point is terribly difficult to determine. Do we grow into a theology of the Word through our own preaching efforts? Or, does our theology of the Word drive our sermon preparation, from exegesis to the actual preaching event? The multiple encounters between Scripture and our theology, between religious traditions and our own human experiences, shape the role of preaching in any congregation. The task, then, of any homiletic method is to take a very intentional approach designed to identify and develop a theology of the Word and to teach us how to wrestle critically with it. Sermon construction emerges from the wrestling "moves" and "holds" that will comprise the preaching event.

I find that many students do not easily understand what homiletic methods actually intend to teach, even if those students are experienced preachers. One pivotal discussion that I have found useful to students stresses that homiletic methods do not supplant or perform the task of discernment. My emphasis lies in helping students discover and exercise the very gifts with which God has called them to be preachers. God seeks to reveal "the Word" for humanity through their preaching. And the work in their part is a discernment activity. Discernment is something they need to pursue through their exegesis, sermon preparation, and their sermon composition—at times, right up to the very moment of delivery. Homiletic methods cannot spare us the labor of discernment. They do not remove the pain of discernment, nor should they suppress the joy of it. Homiletic methods can, however, almost always enhance the discernment task. They give us starting points when we feel blocked; they

give us mapping points when we do not know where to turn; they give us blue prints when we are unsure how to construct. Homiletic methods become partners in the discernment process; the former do not displace the latter.

Teaching African American homiletics presses these tasks a bit further. Our pedagogies in teaching preaching really attempt to help students locate themselves in the process of discernment. The process, of course, is not complete until the student learns to move from the heuristic experience of discernment to the sermon construction and communication of God's revealed Word. However, teaching preaching also emphasizes helping students to understand the components of encounter that go into the preaching event and therefore into sermon preparation. Homiletic methods very much involve skills of argumentation and communication, but within a process of exegesis, discernment, and a re-creation of the "encounter event" that the preacher experienced originally in sermon preparation. James Earl Massey argues that the sermon is designed in the interest of promoting an experience, or a "happening."[2] The homiletic process and the resulting sermon seek to re-create the encounter with God's revelation, but with a selected focus and particular clarity.

An important facet of teaching preaching is to honor the variety of ways of discerning and preaching that students will always bring to the classroom. This facet might just be one of the most difficult elements to sustain in a preaching class, particularly within introductory courses. The difficulty lies in our efforts to give particular attention to methodology among the variety of skills, callings, and experiences. Our task is to teach the use of homiletics methods, all the while helping students explore and encounter the Word for humanity, while learning how they may explore, encounter, and "re-encounter" the Word in the preaching event.

A struggle that often emerges from classroom efforts to introduce students to homiletic methodology involves questions of how purpose informs the process. In some form, these questions ask, "What are we doing when preaching?" One answer is that we are preaching convictions. Another answer suggests that we are preaching passions. Both convictions and passions emerge from the process of exploration and encounter and take shape in sermon composition and in the preaching moment itself. A third answer, which I have grown to prefer, is that preaching is a "meaning making" process. Meaning making is not simply the process, but also the purpose of preaching. Still, all three answers are descriptions that identify the discernment path or discerning encounter in which meaning takes shape.[3] Between sermon construction and the preaching event, a parallel process emerges between encounter and re-encounter in the meaning making process of preaching.

Listening to sermons involves more than the comprehension of an argument. In the black preaching event, one listens for an encounter, whether it is the in-breaking of God's revelation or the healing words of affirmation and confirmation. Certainly, African American preaching has not exclusively cornered the market of encounter in the preaching event. However, the encounter, or an ear to the encounter, becomes a vital component to African American homiletic method and sermon design. We face deep challenges in shaping methodology that will give constructive form to sermons and will co-create the interchange between the anticipated encounter in the preaching event and the encounter driving the sermon preparation process.

Various students experience difficulty with the often noetic interplay in learning black preaching methods between constructing an argument and allowing one's encounter to drive the sermon design. The preacher also wrestles within sermon exploration and preparation to develop a listening ear. Here, the preacher's "listening ear" becomes experiential on many possible levels. We experience an encounter between the sermon's proclamation and our own daily lives; we experience an encounter between God's revelation and our inner lives; we experience an encounter in the preaching moment of God speaking and our hearing, individually yet corporately. Great difficulties thrive in teaching homiletic methods that give sufficient attention to both construction and encounter. Black preaching courses and preaching courses in general struggle with the demands brought by those students who have not yet entered the learning process from experience and encounter. The same courses also struggle under the needs brought by students who are well along the path of the preaching event but not so far along the path of sermon construction designed for bringing the initial encounter to the needed re-encounter.

The future of homiletics will require attention to developing pedagogy that teaches sermon preparation and construction in dialogue with the experiences of "tuning" into the encounter. Homiletics will require attention to developing preachers who listen for an "encounter" in sermon preparation and design. African American homiletics has done well to map the terrain for the preaching encounter. I have called much of this work "homiletic hermeneutics." Homiletic hermeneutics involves interpretation of Scripture, interpretation of church traditions, and interpretation of cultural and historical contexts in which people seek the Word of revelation. African American worship itself is truly worship only when the culture of the congregation drives the hermeneutical process.[4] And it is no less so for black preaching. While culture is not the focal content of the sermon, it is a medium for preaching. Scripture is an immediate criterion for black preaching, but the task is to address people in their culture of language, experience, worldview, and core beliefs.[5] Elsewhere, I have argued that preaching and pastoral care praxis have developed these cultural hermeneutics into ecclesial traditions shaping faith identity between one's personhood and the sense of a peoplehood of God.[6] The hermeneutics of preaching and pastoral care are rooted in some sense of faith identity culled in the encounter of preaching preparation and the re-encounter of the preaching event. Teaching black preaching holds the hermeneutics and experiences of encounter and re-encounter together. ✧

NOTES

1. Fred B. Craddock, *As One Without Authority* (Nashville: Abingdon Press, 979), 133.
2. James Earl Massey, *Designing The Sermon: Order and Movement in Preaching* (Nashville: Abingdon Press, 1980), 20. See also idem, *The Responsible Pulpit* (Anderson, Ind: Warner Press, 1974), 79–80.
3. All three terms emerge out of dialogue with my former colleague, John McClure, and our efforts to revise our basic preaching course in an ongoing endeavor to refocus the use of homiletic methods in sermon preparation.
4. Henry H. Mitchell, "A Brief on Black Worship: Culture and Theology," *American Baptist Quarterly* 5 no. 4 (December 1986): 398.
5. Henry H. Mitchell, *Black Preaching: The Recovery of a Powerful Art* (Nashville: Abingdon Press, 1990), 12.
6. Dale P. Andrews, *Practical Theology for Black Churches: Bridging Black Theology and African American Folk Religion* (Louisville: Westminster John Knox Press, 2002), 31–49.

Church Growth and Management
Advice from the Experts

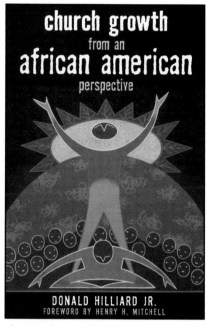

CHURCH GROWTH FROM AN AFRICAN AMERICAN PERSPECTIVE

Order Now!

Bishop Donald Hilliard

"...the approach of this book, if carefully and patiently followed, offers considerable promise."
—DR. HENRY MITCHELL, VISITING PROFESSOR, INTERDENOMINATIONAL THEOLOGICAL CENTER

After taking his congregation from 125 members to more than 7,000 today, Bishop Donald Hilliard shows church leaders how to grow spiritually healthy congregations. He discusses the fundamentals and skillfully points to critical issues such as vision, the centrality of Christ, biblical preaching, sound doctrine, a people-orientation rather than a program-orientation, tithing, and Christian education as necessary for good growth. Each chapter features interactive "action steps" designed to guide leaders from reading the text to doing the text.   0-8170-1495-0 $15.00

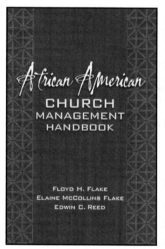

AFRICAN AMERICAN CHURCH MANAGEMENT HANDBOOK

Floyd H. Flake, Elaine McCollins Flake, and Edwin C. Reed

"This book is a valuable resource for churches seeking to do sacred work in secular context."
—MICHAEL A. BATTLE, PRESIDENT, INTERDENOMINATIONAL THEOLOGICAL CENTER

Offering in-depth knowledge and help for churches of ANY denomination and ANY size, this manual covers virtually all aspects of church administration. It may just be the last book on church management a pastor will ever need! Topics include money management, people management, daily operations, the pastor as leader, and much more.   0-8170-1485-3 $15.00

To order call, 800-458-3766 or visit www.judsonpress.com

JUDSON PRESS
PUBLISHERS SINCE 1824

A DANCE MINISTRY in Your Church

DENITA HEDGEMAN

Starting and maintaining an effective dance ministry may sound easy, but it takes spiritual knowledge and maturity, physical skill, awareness of dance routines and varying styles, the ability to recognize dance as a ministry to which persons are called, and dedicated leadership. A dance ministry should be birthed at the leading of the Holy Spirit. Because many churches find this type of ministry startling, the dance ministry leader has to make sure that the ministry follows the mandate and doctrines of the church.

DANCE IN THE SANCTUARY

Some do not believe in dance for the church at all, and these Christians do not have a clue as to where dance is mentioned in the Bible. Others may know that King David danced, but they don't realize just how often dance is mentioned in the Bible. The word dance appears in various forms (danced, dances, dancing, etc.) throughout Scripture, and then there are words related to dancing, such as bow, jump, skip, turn, and leap.

In the Old Testament, dance was typically mentioned concerning worship, celebrations, victory, warfare, festivals, and restoration. In fact, the Hebrew Scripture uses several different words that concern dancing: chiwl, machowl, chagag, halal, yadah, towdah, giyl, karar, raquad, pazaz, alaz, dalag, qaphats, and shiyr. In the New Testament, there are also several Greek words that concern dancing: agalliao, hallomai, exallomai, skirtao, orcheomai, prochoros, and choregeo. In the Gospels and early church, dance was related to celebration, evil or seduction, healing, and faith. The people who danced in the Bible encompass children, women, men, armies, and priests.

I believe that God ordained dance. After-all, in Psalm 150 God tells us to dance specifically in the sanctuary (church)! The Creator created us to praise and worship him through song, dance, drama, poetry, and the preached word. All things were created for God: "For by him were all things created, that are in heaven, and that are in earth, visible and invisible, whether they be thrones, or dominions, or principalities, or powers: all things

Denita Hedgeman is the Minister of Dance at Mississippi Boulevard Christian Church in Memphis, Tennessee.

were created by him, and for him" (Colossians 1:16, KJV).

Unfortunately, even in churches that do embrace the ministry of dance, people do not understand the true purpose of liturgical dance. Too many congregations believe that a dance ministry is an activity that will interest and involve young women—so that these children and youth will stay out of trouble. Other churches form a group simply because dance ministries are in vogue, especially as an attraction to girls. In fact, this association of dance and teenage or preteen girls is so strong that some churches do not want adults to participate in dance ministries; they view such adult involvement as unseemly. These churches do not know that the Bible wants adults, even old men, to dance before the Lord (Jeremiah 31:13). This means that boys and men can dance with all of their might as David did and not worry about it being a ministry most often associated with females. Dance is a part of worship, and everyone was created to worship God.

BEFORE YOU BEGIN

If a dance ministry is to succeed, it is imperative that the pastor, church leaders, minister of music, and minister of dance are all in agreement regarding what God is saying concerning the dance ministry and how God wants it to operate during worship services and as a ministry of the church. All involved need to understand that a dance ministry is established to minister to a congregation, not just to allow persons to perform. A dance should be as powerful as any sermon. It should have a message that is salvific or that lifts up themes such as deliverance, repentance, or praise. A dance routine is most effective when the sermon, Scripture, music, and movement are all focused on the same message.

A dance can be incorporated into any aspect of the service. It may occur during the prelude, the processional, or praise and worship. It can minister during the reading of the Scripture or the collection of tithes and offerings. It may happen during the invitation to Christian discipleship, the altar call, benediction, or recessional. It can even take the place of the sermon. Since liturgical dance occurs during public worship in the Christian church, dance ministries should develop routines for each significant moment of a church's liturgical Christian calendar—for example, the seasons of Lent and Advent, holy days such as Epiphany, Easter, Pentecost, and Christmas, culturally significant events such as Black History Month, Juneteenth, and Kwanzaa, and even major national holidays including Martin Luther King Jr. Day, Mother's and Father's Days, Independence Day, and Thanksgiving Day.

There are a multitude of liturgical dance forms, including praise, congregational, prophetic, warfare, dances of travail, celebration, festive, processional, ceremonial, sermonic, deliverance, altar call, tambourine interpretive, drama, chore-drama, pantomime, and cultural. The dance should always fit the occasion. Dances may be ministered with flags, banners, streamers, ribbons, and billow banners. Types of dance groups include praise dancers, worship dancers, sacred dancers, dance choirs, dance chorales, Davidic dancers, dance dramatists, and dance teams.

WHAT IS REQUIRED OF YOU?

What else is needed to birth a dance ministry in a church? A dance ministry is birthed through intercession and the Holy Spirit. There must be leaders and members of the ministry who are called and anointed for that ministry. Some pastors appoint a leader whom they believe has leadership skills, a knack for working with youth, and/or dance experience and competence. These attributes are needed, but God wants more from a dance ministry leader, as well as from dance team members. Members may want to join the ministry as a public display or because they were blessed and excited by a dance presentation or because their parents want them involved for show; these are superficial reasons to become involved in a dance ministry.

Everyone is called to worship God in dance through praise and worship, but not everyone is called to minister through dance. A calling speaks to a burden or a passion for something—for doing that something. The central call of a liturgical dancer is the deep desire to see souls saved and changed through the power and the anointing that the Holy Spirit gives the dancer as she or he dances. Consistent with that central calling on all members of the dance team, a dance ministry leader must be:

■ A mature, disciplined, steadfast Christian

■ A person who prays, meditates, and allows for the guidance of the Holy Spirit in all aspects of the dance ministry

■ Obedient to pastoral leadership and able to work well with persons in other church ministries

■ Able to establish rules and guidelines for dancers

■ Skillful as a dancer

■ Faithful in the church, having the heart of a servant

■ Committed to the vision of the church and never divisive

■ Able to lead the congregation in worship

■ Organized in performing administrative tasks

■ Passionate about helping others embrace their calling as a liturgical dancer

■ An example for dancers in attending Bible study, praying, and fasting

■ Open to exposing team members to conferences, workshops, master classes, or outreach opportunities.

A member of the dance ministry must be:

■ A Christian and intercessor

■ An active member of the church and enrolled in a biblical studies ministry

■ Committed to placing the will of God and the vision of the church first

■ Submitted to authority and willing to learn

■ Skillful in dance and is a worshiper

■ Punctual and able to follow schedules and dress codes

■ Flexible, consistent, dedicated, and confident

■ Willing to assist others as he or she learns

■ Willing to take classes to improve skills.

Before a dance ministry can begin, the minister of dance needs to know the biblical foundation for dance; what God expects of a liturgical dancer; the pastor's vision regarding the role of a dance ministry in worship; the appropriate church protocol to follow; what types of dances are acceptable and not acceptable in a given church; how different styles of dance can be incorporated into a worship service; how to assess the skill levels of those interested in participating in a dance ministry; and even the type of praise garments (costumes) that will be used.

When it comes to building a team of dancers, a dance leader should consider having auditions to evaluate technical skill. In many cases where teenagers are involved, the leader must assess if the teens are mature enough to be involved in a dance ministry. In some cases, the ministry head might ask potential participants to write an essay concerning their Christian journey and then require them to attend preparatory workshops before they can join the ministry.

It should now be clear that it takes a great deal to begin and sustain a church dance ministry. Pastors and church leaders should be prayerful and prepared before deciding to engage in this type of ministry. However, if the decision is made under the guidance of the Holy Spirit, with the right people and the right protocols and training, then a dance ministry can be a major blessing to any church. ✢

TRAVEL *Eaze*

GROUP TRAVEL CONFERENCE AND EVENT PLANNING

SOUTH AFRICA

Experience the motherland like never before! Only in **South Africa** can you experience radiant sunsets and scenic landscapes, learn more about the struggle against apartheid, and view the freedom of wildlife. This **South Africa** tour covers it all!

Visit the Museums, Soweto, and Johannesburg. Experience a Safari. Spend a day at a township school. A visit to the world-renowned Wandies Restaurant is a must in **Johannesburg.**

During your trip to **Cape Town, South Africa,** you will visit the unforgettable Robben Island, where Nelson Mandela was imprisoned, and take the cable car to Table Mountain.

Departing from **Atlanta**, your sightseeing highlights include: roundtrip airfare from Atlanta, four-star accommodations in **Johannesburg** and **Cape Town**, welcome reception, Sunday worship in the townships, astounding safari and wildlife viewing, educational tours, exciting shopping, elegant breakfast dining, group-chartered air-conditioned motor coach tours, airport transfers, and tips.

This exceptional **12-day South Africa** tour departs **November 9–20, 2006** and is generously priced at **$3,495.00 per person** (US Dollars).

TELL US YOUR DESTINATION, AND WE DO THE REST!

Our expert staff will arrange exclusive group itineraries to suit virtually any category or interest. Relax…Release…and allow **Travel Eaze** to offer you exceptional pricing, worldwide travel, and coordination. **Travel Eaze's** individualized experience takes you away from the ordinary.

Travel Eaze provides superior comfort and efficiency in meeting your needs. Let us assist in making your Conference, Event, or Travel plans a success.

Call or e-mail us today!

TRAVEL EAZE
(Locations in Memphis and Atlanta)

Group Travel, Conference, and Event Planning

Call: 901-526-3364 or
678-571-4135

Fax: 901-528-9476

Email: **traveleaze@msn.com**

Visit us online at:
www.traveleaze.us

An INVISIBLE Calling

The Role of Black Women in the Civil Rights Movement

KAREN JACKSON-WEAVER

A wise teacher's words spur students to action and emphasize important truths.
—Ecclesiastes 12:11, NLT

"Whether I want to do this or not, I got to. This is my calling. This is my mission."
—Fannie Lou Hamer[1]

I began researching the role of black women in the Civil Rights Movement back in 1993. During my archival work, I came across a quote by Fannie Lou Hamer that changed the nature of my project. She explained that her mission was to obtain freedom for all oppressed people, and understanding the risk of losing her life, she likened herself to Esther by declaring, "If I perish, I perish."[2] At that moment I understood that black women's invisible leadership has not only existed since the beginning of time; it was very present and pertinent in the Civil Rights Movement.

Ella Baker, Septima Clark, and Fannie Lou

Karen Jackson-Weaver is the Executive Director of the New Jersey Amistad Commission. In 2005-2006, she was in residence as an Engle Scholar at Princeton Theological Seminary.

Hamer's leadership roles in the Southern Christian Leadership Conference (SCLC), Mississippi Freedom Democratic Party (MFDP), Highlander School, and the Student Non-Violent Coordinating Committee (SNCC) allowed them (and other women in the movement) to share common experiences due to their gender and race. It also enabled them to combine religious beliefs and social activism with education and leadership.

Ella Baker was the first Executive Director of the Southern Christian Leadership Conference (SCLC). This of course has not been emphasized historically, which is surprising since Dr. King led this group of mostly southern black, male ministers. Baker also played a key role in shaping and serving as an advisor to the Student Non-Violent Coordinating Committee (SNCC). Septima Clark was the Director of Workshops and Education at the Highlander Folk School. She also worked closely with Dr. King and Andrew Young on the Board of the SCLC, for which she served as the Director of the Citizenship Education Program. Fannie Lou Hamer was the Vice-Chair of the Mississippi Freedom Democratic Party and a field secretary of SNCC.

All of these positions that they held were quite significant for black women during the late 1950s and early 1960s, and unfortunately the historiography has not highlighted their leadership roles.

Baker, Clark, and Hamer were "called" to these leadership roles during the church-based Civil Rights Movement and struggled to become agents for social and political change while fulfilling God's call to holiness and service to humanity. Though many times relegated to positions of obscurity (which mirrors both the biblical tradition of women being marginalized as found in many of the Old and New Testament narratives and many similar traditions of the black church), these women were still able to make substantial contributions to the full quest for humanity and freedom.

Yes, Ella Baker, Septima Clark, and Fannie Lou Hamer emerge as leaders of the Civil Rights Movement despite the patriarchal and racist systems they encountered within the "black church" tradition. They were able to overcome this deeply entrenched marginalization, racism, and sexism by using their religious heritage, training, and upbringing to bring about equal treatment for communal and societal good. Additionally, they personified various meanings of leadership, particularly as it relates to women. Despite their marginalization, they remained dedicated and active, even if it meant not being at the forefront of the movement. Baker, Clark, and Hamer realized they were called by God, and as a result they understood they were accountable to a Supreme Being—not a human one.

Their model of leadership is based on a servant-leadership paradigm. This type of leadership is rooted in biblical tradition and mirrors the experiences of biblical figures such as Miriam, the sister of Moses and Aaron;

Esther, a Hebrew queen; and Jochebed, the mother of Moses, Aaron, and Miriam. My research builds upon that of other scholars, such as Dr. Rosetta Ross, who argues that the civil rights historiography emphasizes moral values versus religious values, culture, and influences. When it does explore religious values and influences, this exploration is done primarily utilizing a male's perspective.

The complex nature of black women's leadership in the Civil Rights Movement has historically significant issues with modern social policy implications. One of the central tenets of my study has explored how the activism of black women reflects a unique orientation to the process of political organizing for the purpose of changing social policy.[3] Baker, Clark, and Hamer's use of grassroots indigenous leadership as a means to bring about literacy, voter registration, and community leadership resulted in significant policy changes. It also allowed them to fulfill their God-given mission on multiple levels and embrace "the call."

Baker, Clark, and Hamer's revolutionary work was not done simply to change laws. They sought to dismantle separatist legal regimes and empower communities with access to education, economic, and sociopolitical opportunities while fighting the systemic, vigilante violence of whites who embraced racist notions and supremacist ideologies. Within the framework of this struggle, black women were facing the challenges of being both black and female. Therefore, a quiet women's revolution was unfolding in the midst of the struggle for black freedom and liberation. As a result, activists like Baker, Clark, and Hamer came to critique the nature of gender relations in the black community for reinforcing the same patriarchy that the white society embraced. Instead of copying a flawed model, black women leaders sought to examine gender relations and create a godly model in which both black men *and* black women could both be fully human.[4] They understood and embraced that "God created male and female in his image and it was very good."[5]

Septima Clark recognized that much of the literature on the Civil Rights Movement focused on the role of men and their leadership and that consequently women were not acknowledged for their efforts. "In stories about the civil rights movement you hear mostly about the black ministers. But if you talk to the women who were there, you'll hear another story. I think the civil rights movement would never have taken off if some women hadn't started to speak up. A lot more are just getting to the place now where they can speak out."[6]

Baker, Clark, and Hamer were not just "bridge" leaders, organizers, activists, or workers as other scholars have proposed. In fact, one might argue that these labels are reductionist descriptors. These women were leaders who were restricted from being "out front" because of their race and gender—and, in Fannie Lou Hamer's case, possibly because of their class and educational background.

Another possible explanation for the lack of recognition in civil rights literature for Baker, Clark, and Hamer as leaders could be the normative, systematic oppression and omission of black women in sociopolitical analysis. Teresa Nance argues that "social science research typically focuses on the public, official, visible political activity even though the unofficial, private, and seemingly invisible sphere of social life and organization may be equally important." One of the first notions that must be challenged is what constitutes (or what defines) significant contributions to a social movement.[7] Because black women like

Baker, Clark, and Hamer were engaged in the grassroots, Southern black freedom struggle, they were not able to generate the kind of rhetorical artifacts (e.g., policy statements, public speeches) that would have catapulted their names or words into print.[8]

It is imperative that we freedom fighters who share the gospel with others learn the valuable lessons from the experiences of Baker, Clark, and Hamer, as well as from the experiences of their biblical sisters. We must learn from the past and explore the modern day implications. Baker, Clark, and Hamer were not just leaders; they were ministers. *Easton's Bible Dictionary* defines a minister as "one who serves." These women, and indeed many countless, nameless others, had a tremendous impact on every individual they encountered. Unfortunately, they were not officially recognized as ministers or leaders. But there are words from the pen of the hymnwriter Lucie Campbell that give us hope for these women—and even for ourselves: "If when you give the best of your service, telling the world that the Savior is come, Be not dismayed when men don't believe you. He'll understand and say 'Well Done.'"[9]   ✤

NOTES

1. Quoted in Kay Mills, *This Little Light of Mine* (Plume Books New York, 1983), 113.
2. Esther 4:16, NIV.
3. Teresa A. Nance, "Hearing the Missing Voice," in *Journal of Black Studies*, 26, no. 5 (May 1996): 543–59.
4. My discussions with Dr. Manning Marable and the literature on black women activists were helpful in making these arguments.
5. Genesis 1:27, 31, NLT.
6. Cynthia Stokes Brown, ed., *Ready from Within: Septima Clark and the Civil Rights Movement* (Navarro, CA: Wild Tress Press, 1986), 83.
7. Brown, 83.
8. Teresa Nance highlights this argument in her article as well.
9. "He'll Understand and Say 'Well Done.'" Lyrics by Lucie E. Campbell (GIA Publications, Inc., 2000).

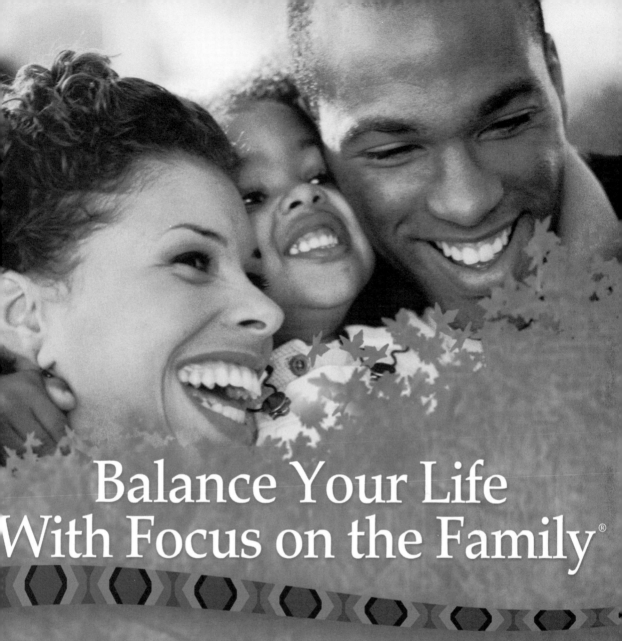

Balance Your Life
With Focus on the Family®

ocus on the Family Magazine
's everything that surrounds your family. Inside
ach issue, you'll find articles on marriage, life
ages, childrearing, Christian growth and current
ssues. When you're working hard to keep everything
ogether in our ever-changing culture, the resources
nd encouragement provided can be a big help.

he Pastoral Care Line
his is our support and crisis phone line for pastors
nd their families. It features a staff of pastors who

can provide an understanding ear, a word of advice,
a timely referral or thoughtful prayer.

Gatekeepers
We have an opportunity for you to reach out to
your congregation and community. By becoming a
Gatekeeper, you can help us increase the awareness
of resources available to African-Americans. With
your partnership, we can further meet the needs of
the people you care about most.

Focus on the Family
African-American Outreach
(719) 531-3360
Toll-free Pastoral Care Line (877) 233-4455
www.family.org/pastor/aa

FOCUS ON THE FAMILY
PASTORAL MINISTRIES

PI06FAAAP

Preaching Faith to HEAL THEM

W. W. Austin (1885–1931) and the Origins of the North Sixth Street Church of God in Christ

ELTON H. WEAVER III

THE AFRICAN AMERICAN**PULPIT** FALL 2006

Pastor William Wallace Austin was a faith healer[1] and one of the Church of God in Christ's (COGIC) pioneering pastors. He evangelized the southeastern bootheel of Missouri and established one of the first COGIC churches in the country, North Sixth Street COGIC.

Austin was born on March 21, 1885, in Smith County, Mississippi. The son of former

Elton H. Weaver III is a candidate for the Ph.D. in history at the University of Memphis, Tennessee. His dissertation focuses on the life and times of Bishop C. H. Mason, founder of the Church of God in Christ (COGIC).

slaves Tobe and Bessie Austin, he was raised in the African American Christian Methodist Episcopal Church (CME).[2] When Austin was a child, his mother was stricken with an illness, and because of the low tenant farming wages his father earned, the family could not afford proper medical care. When a doctor finally arrived, nothing could be done to prevent Bessie from dying. Austin was only nine years old, and the early loss of his mother had a lasting effect on his life. He grew up wishing he had had power to cure his mother. After his father remarried, the family relocated to Crystal Springs, Mississippi. Austin himself later married and had a daughter whom he named Bessie Elizabeth, but soon after that tragedy struck again. This time he lost his wife to a fatal illness. After his wife's death Austin fell into a depressed state, agonizing about not being able to do anything to prevent her death and wondering how he would be able to raise a daughter alone.

When Austin was in his twenties, Bishop Charles H. Mason came to Crystal Springs and conducted an open-air revival. During that meeting Austin embraced Mason's movement. As Austin's sister recalled, "My brother heard Bishop Mason preaching in a wagon and joined up with him and later became a preacher in the Church of God in Christ."[3] After being exposed to Mason's brush arbor meetings, four things caused Austin to join Mason's movement: the people, the praise, the preaching, and the power. **People** from every walk of life were welcomed and came to be renewed during the revival. This was because Mason's message touched the lives of the poor working classes, and his ability to connect with them caused rural people to flock to his meetings as well.

Mason's services were also very lively, and **praise** was allowed and encouraged. In the CME church of Austin's youth, they too had praised God, but most of the praise at that time revolved around the Methodist hymnals.

Poor black tenant farmers could relate to Mason's **preaching** concerning God's bondage-breaking power. In Mason's demonstrations he often used a potato held in bondage by a small iron rivet. When Mason spoke he assured the people that God would free them from their bondage. He said, "The band of oppression around you, God is able to break."[4] Austin was especially attracted to what Mason said about healing. "The Lord healeth all our diseases," cried Mason. "The Lord brings health and cure to those who are sick and oppressed. He gave healing power to

his disciples and to them that believe. The Spirit's gift in the churches is to heal."[5]

Austin observed numerous *demonstrations* of that healing **power**. People who were sick with illnesses such as the ones that had caused Austin's mother's and wife's deaths came to Mason. He anointed them with oil and laid hands on them, and many testified they had been healed by the power of God.

After receiving ordination through the COGIC, Austin heard God asking him to carry the gospel to the state of Missouri. Despite the disapproval of his family, Austin packed up his daughter and headed out to the border state.

Austin reached Missouri in the 1910s and settled in Pemiscot County. When he arrived he discovered that the southeastern bootheel of Missouri had not been evangelized. Therefore he set out to evangelize it.[6] Soon after his arrival he met and married a widow named Julia Kaufman. After they were married, he and Julia started evangelizing the bootheel together. Initially Austin held services from house-to-house and in the brush arbors of Canady, but his membership grew and Mason sent word for Austin to establish a COGIC congregation in the city of Hayti. It was in the 1910s when Austin established the North Sixth Street COGIC. He also continued evangelizing blacks living in the rural bootheel communities. His message reached those who were unable to travel to the city. After several years of rural evangelism, Austin's church gained several hundred members.

Between 1910 and 1930 thousands of blacks migrated to the bootheel. Landowners hired them to pick cotton and dig ditches in order to drain the swamps that covered the lowlands. Austin preached to black migrants, and they were the people who joined his church. He preached to blacks and whites living in Hayti, Canady, Caruthersville, and

Micola. Mother Isadore Rainey, one of Austin's surviving church members, said that Austin was a faith healer and that God gave him the gift of healing:

> At that time Pemiscot County was covered in swamps, and I caught typhoid fever and the fever would not go away. My husband could not afford a doctor and everyone thought I was going to die. Someone in the house said, "Call Pastor Austin." Pastor Austin drove an old Model T Ford and would often make house calls to the sick and shut-in. He carried a doctor's bag but was not a medical doctor. He carried a bottle of anointed oil and a Bible in his bag. When he came in my room, he anointed my body with oil, laid his hands on me, and prayed for God to heal me. Several hours later the fever left and I recovered.[7]

Like Mason, Austin embraced the black healing tradition and fought to cure black people suffering from physical and psychological traumas.

In Pemiscot, Austin encountered bootheel racism. Poor white workers resented black migrants; they were threatened by the presence of the migrants and blamed blacks for their own unemployment, low wages, and high rents.[8] In fact, black workers were beaten, run off lands, and lynched by nightriders in the struggle for economic control. Blacks who fought back suffered physical injuries and psychological distress. During the racial conflicts, Austin was right there to help heal the pain. He and his wife tended those who had been beaten and preached messages of comfort, speaking words such as, "What's done in the dark will be brought to light" and "Fight the good fight," and singing songs such as, "I am going through. If Jesus takes me through, I'll pay the price whatever others may do; I started with Jesus, and I am going through."

Austin openly opposed violent acts aimed against black people. One night, after conducting a revival in Micola, he was warned by a band of nightriders that if he continued to "keep them niggers out too late you will end up dead."[9] Their threats did not stop Austin; he kept right on preaching revivals and holding late-night services. After being warned several more times to leave the state of Missouri, Austin told his family, "God sent me to the bootheel and no one is going to run me off."[10] By 1926 North Sixth Street COGIC was thriving, and Austin's name was listed in COGIC's annual "Pastor's Church Report."[11]

In 1931, while riding in a wagon headed to preach in the bootheel, Austin was struck by a white driver. When the wagon was hit, Austin was thrust from the wagon and later died at his house. Authorities ruled his death an accident, but witnesses, church members, and Austin's family knew that his death was no accident. They believed that the whites of Hayti followed through with their threats to kill Austin.

Today Austin's North Sixth Street COGIC is more than ninety years old. Austin and early COGIC pioneers sought to eradicate the socioeconomic and psychological problems blacks experienced in twentieth-century America by showing blacks how to believe in a higher power. Pastor Nathaniel Ellis, North Sixth Street's current pastor, said that Austin's church is COGIC's "Mother Church" in southeastern Missouri, and most COGIC churches in the area sprouted out of Austin's church.[12] In a recent proclamation, Bishop Gilbert Earl Patterson, presiding prelate of COGIC, recognized and thanked North Sixth Street COGIC for decades of faithful service. He declared, "Many can attest that the ministry of North Sixth Street COGIC has been a source of comfort, guidance, healing, and strength. You have a glorious past and a promising future."[13]

Austin and the development of his church is crucial in our understanding of the black healing tradition in America and sheds light on the historical growth of ethnomedicine and how it functioned and served blacks in a racist and class-based society. Austin was a leader and healer of the African American community. He surmounted racial opposition, evangelized the southeastern bootheel of Missouri, and established one of the oldest COGIC churches in the country.   ✤

NOTES

1. Zora N. Hurston. "Hoodoo in America." *Journal of American Folklore*, issue 44 (October–December, 1931), 317–417. Z. N. Hurston. *The Sanctified Church* (Berkeley, CA: Turtle Island, 1981). Hans A. Baer. "Toward a Systematic Typology of Black Folk Healers." *Phylon*, vol. 43, no. 4 (1982), 327–43.

2. Othal H. Lakey. *The Rise of Colored Methodism* (Dallas, TX: Crescendo Book Publications, 1972).

3. William Wallace Austin was my great-great-grandfather on my mother's side. My mother's people are from Smith County, Mississippi. During slavery they embraced the Methodist faith. Austin Family Bible; Beulah Austin Sydnor, "Grandpa Austin." Oral Interview (Gary, Indiana, 1996).

4. Charles H. Mason. "God Will Break You Out of Bondage" in *Sermons from the Life of Bishop C. H. Mason* (Memphis, TN: n.d.).

5. Charles H. Mason. "The Lord Healeth" in *Sermons from the Life of Bishop C. H. Mason* (Memphis, TN: n.d.).

6. Luther B. Williams. "The Church of God in Christ of St. Louis, Missouri: its early stages and its early developments." Oral interview (St. Louis, MO: n.d.). Dupree Afro-Pentecostal Collection, History of Missouri COGIC in the Schomburg Center for Research in Black Culture, Harlem, New York. Charles H. Pleas, *Fifty Years Achievement History of the Church of God in Christ* (Memphis, TN: 1955), n.p.; Elijah L. Hill, "Bishop V. M. Barker" in *Women Come Alive* (Arlington, TX: Perfecting the Kingdom International Ministries, Co., 2005), 86–101.

7. Isadore Rainey. "Pastor Austin and the North Six Street COGIC." Oral interview (Hayti, MO: 2005).

8. Jarod H. Roll. "From Revolution to Reaction: Early Pentecostalism, Radicalism, and Race in Southeast Missouri, 1910–1930." *Radical History Review*, issue 90 (fall 2004): 5–30. Irvin G. Wyllie, "Race and Class Conflict on Missouri's Cotton Frontier." *The Journal of Southern History*, vol. 20, no. 2 (May 1954): 183–96; Hugh Denney, "Boot Heel Regional Profile," Department of Regional and Community Affairs Extensions Division (University of Missouri Special Collections, Columbia, MO).

9. Beulah Austin Sydnor, "Grandpa Austin." Oral Interview (Gary, IN: 1996).

10. B. A. Sydnor, Interview, 1996.

11. Lillian B. Coffey. *Year Book for the Church of God in Christ for the Year 1926* (Chicago, IL: 1926).

12. Nathaniel Ellis. "North Sixth Street Past and Present." Oral interview (Hayti, MO: 2005).

13. Gilbert Earl Patterson. "Letter to National Evangelist Nathaniel A. Ellis and North Sixth Street COGIC." Office of the Presiding Bishop (Memphis, TN: 2000). *In Celebration of Our Eighty-six Plus Years North Sixth Street Church of God in Christ Program and Souvenir Journal* (Hayti, MO: Sunday, October 16, 2005).

WHY SEEK Ye the Living among the Dead?

JACQUELINE BLUE

Luke 24:1-5, KJV

Now upon the first day of the week, very early in the morning, they came unto the sepulcher, bringing the spices which they had prepared, and certain others with them. And they found the stone rolled away from the sepulcher....[The angels] said unto them, Why seek ye the living among the dead? (Luke 24:1-2,5b)

On this second Sunday in May, we have entered a time of the Christian year designated as Ordinary Time. We began at Advent with the longing, seeking, and hoping

Jacqueline Blue is a 2006 Master of Divinity graduate of Phillips Theological Seminary in Tulsa, Oklahoma. She serves as minister of Christian education at St. James Missionary Baptist Church in Fayetteville, Arkansas.

for the Christ child. As we immersed ourselves in the reality of Emmanuel, God with us, we did so with the premature pains of the weight of the cross that we knew would soon be birthed into our future.

Then the season of Lent facilitated a careful and methodical approach to the cross. Lent is a time set aside to understand the meaning of the term *sacrifice* in its totality. Through Lent, the hope is that the resurrection becomes more than an opportunity to color eggs, purchase new clothes, and make an annual church appearance. Lent is a forty-day progressive walk to what I have deemed as the highest holy day of the year—Easter. During this walk toward Easter, we affirm the pain of the cross and at the same time the limitless love of God that reaches through that pain, lifts each of us out of ourselves, and gives us a place of grace. This grace is not one that can be achieved, but one that must be bestowed.

Then on our calendar, the disillusionment of the cross ultimately gives way to the beginning of the first church, soon after the celebration of Pentecost. It was on Pentecost that the people of God found their voice. They discovered that Jesus was real and that his word was true. On the day of Pentecost, fifty days after the resurrection, we remember how the Spirit of the Living God fell and how that Spirit now dwells among us.

However, today is the forty-third day after the resurrection and nothing is going on. That is why it is called "Ordinary Time." It's just one normal day after the next. Jesus is gone, the disciples are confused, the followers have no one to follow; it just seems ordinary.

Do you have any days when nothing is happening? Where it seems as though a minute lasts an hour, when your desire is for the present day to pass in hopes that a new, more exciting day comes?

Let me challenge your thinking. God does his best work when it seems that nothing out of the ordinary is going on. Don't believe me; ask the centurion at the foot of the cross.

Crucifixion was an ordinary thing for him. He witnessed such executions day in and day out, but when Jesus was crucified, he received an *extra*ordinary revelation, so much so that he said: "Surely this was the Son of God."[1]

Need another witness? Consult Jesus. As he was traveling to the house of Jairus to heal that man's daughter, a woman touched the hem of his garment. Not only was she healed, but Jesus cried out, "Who touched me?"[2] What began as ordinary ended in extraordinary blessings. Have you had any of these? Extraordinary blessings, just out of nowhere blessed.

Today is Mother's Day. We have one every year. We repeat the same rituals every year. And it is customary for most mothers to receive some form of gift, every year. Nothing unexpected happens; it's just another ordinary day.

Women are one of God's extraordinary creations. We are indeed the cat's meow and humanity's bow-wow. With a glance, we can stop traffic, and with just one look, we can issue a full sermonic hymn without uttering a word. And all the children say, "Amen!"

Stored within us is the strength to carry the weight of the world, the compassion to nurse it through the toughest of times, the foreknowledge to predict catastrophic events, and a memory to recall each and every occurrence. Women serve in a variety of positions in life. We are wives, mothers, sisters, aunties, grandmothers, teachers, doctors, nurses, social workers, ushers, Sunday school teachers, choir members, deacons, elders, ministers, and pastors. In every facet of life, you will find a woman. Can you imagine a world without the face or presence of women?

God gave his best when he created the woman. Nevertheless, even with all the goodness, grace, and divine inspiration, we women have figured out a way to misappropriate the use of one of our abilities. That ability is called our memory; we have the ability to hang on to our past. For some peculiar reason, we do not forget a thing, especially if it falls in the realm of emotion. Directly linked to this *ability* is our *in*ability to move on because of what we remember. If we just learn to let it go, life would be much sweeter. Instead, we remember, we hold on, we stand still, and we look back. In essence, we become walking tombs carrying our dead past experiences with us.

If we are honest with ourselves, each of us brought our own private tomb with us today. Some tombs are small because our life experiences have been few or because some of us are actively working to move on in life. Others of us brought large tombs because our coping skills have not been sharpened and self-preservation is the only tool being used. As a result, every experience is carefully and neatly arranged in the tomb so that it can be visited and reflected upon on a regular basis.

Not only do we have this tomb within us, but we have carefully learned how to hide it from public view—and in some cases, even from ourselves. We have learned through the years how to dress properly to cover the hurt, how to shout on cue to make it seem like all is well, or how to cook the perfect meal to mask the lack of words to verbalize the pain. Is this a science that only women are privy to? Is it just the women?

What is it that keeps us hanging on to those failures, hurts, and disappointments? What is it that makes us more comfortable with our dead past experiences instead of live people who love us? Why would we rather shield ourselves in the tomb than live life to its fullest? What happened to cause us to lose a measure of our God-given hope? Why has carrying our past with us become an ordinary part of our lives? Could it be that we feel safe surrounded by our past experiences?

It seems as though when we need real company, we go to the tomb. When we need real understanding, we go to the tomb. When we need a hiding place, we go to the tomb.

If we go to our tombs, we know exactly what to expect. The sting of the hurt has already occurred, the disappointments are past, and the lack of compassion has been felt. In essence, we are safe because we know what is there. But I would suggest the very thing that provides safety is preventing us from moving forward.

As we turn to the text, the Marys have something to teach women. We notice they are preparing a burial ritual. The fact that this is a burial ritual suggests only one thing: something or someone is dead! *Dead*, an adjective meaning "no longer living; without

life; lacking warmth, interest, brightness; without feeling, motion, or power." *Dead*. This was the state of the body they were preparing to see. This is also the state of those past experiences we are hanging on to.

The process or ritual of preparing the spices was a normal occurrence for the women. It was passed down to them through the ages. I would imagine it was something they had watched their mothers do time and time again. Just like the Marys, we have had years of preparation, of learning how to store our hurts and appear as if all were well, in spite of dying on the inside.

Notice, the women pay careful attention to ensure that they have enough perfume and spices to cover the stench of death. The Gospel of John tells us that seventy-five pounds of myrrh and aloe were used when the body was initially placed in the tomb,[3] but the women purchased more.

Are we much different than they? The perfume and spices we use today take on multiple forms. We cover our private tombs with clothes, busy schedules, titles, homes, cars, friends, children…the list is endless. At the end of the day, all of our efforts have only masked the stench of what lies within us.

Next we notice that the Marys start out early in the morning on a long journey to the tomb. They carry with them despondency, discouragement, and hopelessness. The only thing that remained was this one final task. After its completion, back to the ordinary way of life. Can't you see them as they walk? The one in whom they had placed their hope was crucified; the one who had spoken against the rulers of the day was crucified; the one who had given them a reason to look forward to tomorrow was crucified.

We can walk right alongside the Marys as they take this walk. But then there is a cruel twist to this narrative. When the Marys arrive, the stone covering the tomb is not there. In my mind, I can only imagine the sheer terror. If we could get into their minds, we'd hear them thinking: "The one place where I kept my secrets safe is now wide open. The one thing that kept me safe is no longer there. My protective covering is now gone." All of a sudden, what was once an ordinary state of being had shifted in the blink of an eye and they were exposed.

I imagine that I am suddenly just as exposed—my private tomb open to any random passerby. The possibility that people will really know who I am has just become real. What will they think when they find out that I have issues? Will I no longer be a part of the group? Am I good enough to be invited back? Oh my goodness, what do people know about me? These questions plague my mind as I stand and face my open tomb. What about you? What questions do you have?

Despite finding themselves exposed, the Marys do not stop there. They drag us past our fears into a new but not *so* new reality. As they enter the tomb, they are silent. They look and look and look. I run behind them into the tomb, and I look in the section of the tomb that kept my regrets hidden safely away. I look in the drawer labeled "attempted suicide," but the drawer is empty. I pull open the drawer labeled "abortion," but it is empty. When I surveyed my regrets about not attending college, finishing high school, or getting a GED, all three drawers are empty.

After finding nothing in the regrets area, I frantically move to the center of the tomb that housed my disappointments. I yank open the drawer marked "lack of acknowledgment," where I kept the pain of all the times I was looked over and no one considered my feelings. But this drawer is empty too. "Failed relationships," empty; "spouse up and left," empty; "parents gave me away," empty.

I do not know what to do, so I continue searching because I do not think I can live without the comfort of my tomb. I rush to the right where I kept my guilt. I search through the drawer of "divorce," empty; "incest," empty; "low self-esteem," empty; "unresolved deaths," empty.

There is one final hope, and I cling to it as I face the final space in the room. It is there that I look to the wall of failure. Slowly, I approach the drawer labeled "family dysfunction," empty; "depression," empty; "bankruptcy," empty; "children on drugs," empty; "children incarcerated," empty; "not on speaking terms with my children," empty.

Defeated and exposed, it is then that I hear a question that shakes my very foundation: "Why seek ye the living among the dead?"

All the stuff that I had carried was dead, but I was alive. Jesus, the one I said I trusted, took all the dead past experiences so that I could live. I came to the realization that I did not trust him with the stuff in my tomb, but just as the Marys found the tomb empty, Jesus has emptied my tomb. Jesus has also emptied your tomb, and we must get to the place where we trust that the work Jesus has performed is done. And when he did it, it was done *completely*.

As I go to my seat, there is a hymn of meditation I would invite the women to join me in singing. It begins, "'Tis so sweet to trust in Jesus, just to take him at his word, just to rest upon his promises, just to know 'Thus saith the Lord.'"[4] It is in trusting him that we leave all the baggage of the past and live the life that God has ordained for us—an extraordinary life in an ordinary time. ✦

NOTES

1. Matthew 27:54, KJV. All Scriptures in this sermon are quoted from the King James Version.
2. Mark 5:22-30.
3. John 19:39.
4. "'Tis So Sweet to Trust in Jesus," words by Louisa M. R. Stead, 1882.

THE AFRICAN AMERICAN**PULPIT** FALL 2006

2nd

By WHOSE Authority Do You Preach?

CHRISTOPHER M. JONES

1 Kings 19:1-8, KJV

And the angel of the Lord came again the second time, and touched him, and said, Arise and eat; because the journey is too great for

Christopher M. Jones is a Master of Divinity student at Princeton Theological Seminary in Princeton, New Jersey. He serves as pastoral liaison and elder-elect to the Cathedral International Church of Perth Amboy, New Jersey.

thee. And he arose, and did eat and drink, and went in the strength of that meat forty days and forty nights unto Horeb the mount of God. (1 Kings 19:7-8)

It has been several days now since the cow-dung-slinging prophet, Elijah of Tishbe, had encountered the evil words of Jezebel, delivered through the mouth of a messenger. In essence, Jezebel sent word to Elijah saying, "I am going to crack your skull and spread its fragments from the banks of the Euphrates all the way to the sandy dunes of the Upper Nile River! The next time that I encounter your big prophesying mouth, I am going to destroy you, any residue of your prophetic decrees, and the God whom you proclaim to serve! Elijah, the next time that you see my face, you and your bipolar disposition—standing for God one day, hiding under a tree the next—let the gods do to me, and more also, if I make not thy life as the life of them [slain prophets of Baal] by tomorrow about this time."

This kind of message would shake even you. It was as if Jezebel were saying to the prophet: "Elijah, by whose authority have you chosen to bring down fire? By whose authority do you disseminate rebuke, prophetic instruction, and bring correction to the royal office of my husband, King Ahab? By whose authority do you talk about faith as being the substance of things hoped for, and the evidence of things not yet seen? By whose authority, Elijah? Who do you think you are?"

So here we are. The stage has been set. It doesn't take long, my brothers and sisters, to contemplate the complexity of Elijah's crisis. "By whose authority do you preach?" This is the million dollar qualitative question implied in Jezebel's death threat to Elijah. In the previous chapter, Elijah was used by God to pass judgment on those who worshiped the deity called Baal. Upon receiving the word that Elijah had started a revival, Jezebel sent notice that Elijah would be dead in a day. Elijah jumped in his hoopty with spinning 20-inch rims, dropped off his armor bearer in Beersheba, ditched the license plates, hid the honorarium, and parked in the wilderness under a juniper tree, ready to die.

Indeed, Elijah had been called by God to bring a sure-fire revival to northern Israel, to kill a devil, and to preach prophetically. And yet, we now find our brother Elijah in the midst of conflict, pressing to find a balanced perspective in God's purpose for his life. Dr. H. Beecher Hicks defined such agony as being akin to a preacher "desiring physical suicide" as opposed to "delayed homicide."[1] Hear this. Jezebel said, "I heard what you did, preacher! You'll be dead by tomorrow!" Elijah paused, looked toward the Lord, and said, "Just kill me right now. I can't take the pressure of preaching in the prophetic anymore. I am tired of you nudging me to speak truth to power, to bring revival to a people who do not love you, and to make prophetic decrees to a brother stuck in his situation, dead in his disposition, and chained to his circumstance. Lord, you can kill me right now! I can't take it anymore!" Floundering in his flow, one could say Elijah had become temporarily cut off from his calling, choosing to embrace death over deliverance.

To be sure, if we are going to preach in the prophetic, we must come to the realization that there will be times in our life when we will feel like dying rather than preaching. What do I mean? Behold, Elijah, the prophet from Tishbe, called to preach the devil out of God's people, yet not strong enough to handle harsh ridicule. Called to manipulate the elements in the atmosphere with a spoken word, yet not strong enough to master the dysfunction of his own psychological depression. Called to bring down revival fire from God, yet not strong enough to keep his own fire burning. Called to push God's people toward their place of purpose and destiny, yet not strong enough to press beyond his issue in isolation.

Elijah, in all his frailty, told God, "Kill me right now! I can't take the pressure anymore. Yesterday I was your Bout-it Bout-it No-Limit Soldier, but today I can't see beyond my circumstance. Yesterday I had your people shouting hallelujah at the revival, but today I am faking the funk in flunk city. Yesterday I lifted up mine eyes toward the hills from which cometh my help, but today the only thing that I want to lift is a gun to my head! The way that I feel right now, God, I would rather die than preach in the prophetic! I would rather shut up than let your Holy Spirit show out! Lord, kill me right now! I can't take it anymore!"

Everybody walks with a little bit of Elijah on the inside every once in awhile. I'm referring to those days when we walk with more fear than faith, more pain than prayer, more depression than discipline, and more paranoia than patience. By whose authority do you preach when you shift from serving at the pinnacle of ministerial success, to living in a dark valley filled with despair? By whose authority do you preach when you call down revival fire one day, and the next

Everybody walks with a little bit of Elijah on the inside every once in awhile…with more fear than faith, more pain than prayer, more depression than discipline, and more paranoia than patience.

day somebody is talking about you, your ministry, your mission, and your momma? By whose authority do you preach when the oil overflowed yesterday, but today you don't have a word, your ministry dried up, and the bank threatened to close the doors and put a padlock on? By whose authority do you preach, Elijah?

By whose authority do you preach when the church sits down on your vision, the marriage loses its testimony, the doctor says it's terminal, and you've got thirty days until your eviction? No "hallelujah." No "thank you, Lord." No "come back and preach again." No "I love you." No "your better days are yet to come." You've become depressed and dysfunctional, seemingly cut off from the Comforter who keeps you. In fact, you told the Lord, "We can shut this preaching thing down right now!"

But, the pericope continues. "And as he lay and slept under a juniper tree, behold, then an angel touched him, and said unto him, Arise and eat." Don't you know that the love of God will locate you in the midst of your circumstance? God will send an angel to pick you up right when you want to sit down. If we are going to preach prophetically, we must come to the realization that we are not alone. Yes, there will be days when we will feel like dying, but we have to know that we are not alone. God, in God's propensity to supply our every need according to God's riches in glory, will always send a confirming word and a helping hand to lift us from our

place of paralysis to point us toward our destiny with God. You've got to move beyond human affirmation and focus on the God who touched you. You've got to move beyond your own despair and set your eyes on the God who called you, spoke to you, and blessed you.

God is faithful. God will always send you help when you need it. Somebody will always have a word, a hand, or a hallelujah to get you through! Yes, we are often concerned with whether or not we can preach in the prophetic—the unapologetic Word of the Lord, in the midst of despair. Yes, there are forces out there that are opposed to the will of God for your life. However, we must remember that God will sustain us in God's timeliness. It's the timely God-ordained encounter that enables us to keep preaching!

The angel of God said to Elijah, "Arise and eat." In other words, "Elijah, you have completed one segment of the journey, but there is yet more to come. I affirm you. Be encouraged. I love you. You are not alone. Elijah, you were faithful in the last assignment, but arise and eat! God is not through with you yet! Elijah, heaven is concerned about you! Arise and eat! You have back-up Elijah! Don't you know who is in control of your destiny? Don't you know by whose authority you preach?"

On one side, Jezebel challenges Elijah's authority through the proclamation of death. On the other side, the angel of the Lord challenges Elijah's authority through the procla-

Do we preach unto death or do we preach unto life? Do we preach under our own power? Or do we preach under the power of the living God who sent us?

mation of life. Do we preach unto death or do we preach unto life? Do we preach under our own power? Or do we preach under the power of the living God who sent us?

God's messenger reminds Elijah whose power he preaches under. He tells him, "Don't you know that no weapon formed against you will prosper? Get up from under your juniper tree, Elijah! Get up from depression! Get up from self-doubt! Get up from your defeatist mindset! Not by your might, Elijah. Not by your strength but by the spirit of the Lord will the Word of God yet prosper in your mouth!"

"And the angel of the Lord came again the second time, and touched him, and said, Arise and eat; because the journey is too great for thee. And he arose, and did eat and drink, and went in the strength of that meat forty days and forty nights unto Horeb the mount of God." Know this, today's Elijahs. If we are going to preach in the prophetic, we must come to the realization that God will equip us and empower us to finish what we have started. Yes, there will be days that we will feel like dying more than preaching. But God will equip us and empower us to finish what we have started! The Bible tells us that Elijah *did* eat and drink and went in the strength of that meat. In other words, not only did God meet Elijah in his place of paralysis, but God shifted Elijah's perspective from dysfunction to destiny. In other words, "They that wait upon the Lord shall renew their strength, they shall mount up with wings as eagles; they shall run, and not

be weary; and they shall walk and not faint."[2] "The Lord is good, a strong hold in the day of trouble, and he knoweth them that trust in him."[3] "Weeping may endure for a night, but joy cometh in the morning."[4] Elijah *went in the strength of that meat for forty days and forty nights.* Translation: God will equip us and empower us to finish what we have started.

The cosmic judge is still raising the question—by whose authority do you preach? The Bible suggests that Elijah answered this way. He dusted himself off, jumped back in his hoopty, and went on to his next assignment at Mt. Horeb. In other words, he was saying, I preach by the authority of the God who created and sustained me— the Alpha and the Omega, the beginning and the end! This is the good news, preachers! We can continue to be prophetic knowing that yes, there will be some dark days. However, we are not alone. God will empower us and equip us to complete what we have started! We serve a God who will supply our every need! In the midst of disrespect, depression, and dysfunction, we have been called to preach in the prophetic in this present age! By whose authority do you preach? Say with certainty: By the authority of Almighty God! ✢

NOTES

1. H. Beecher Hicks Jr. *Preaching through a Storm* (Grand Rapids, MI: Zondervan Publishing House 1987), 129.
2. Isaiah 40:31.
3. Nahum 1:7.
4. Psalm 30:5.

THE HOPE in His Holler

3rd

MALENE S. MINOR

Luke 23:46, NRSV

Then Jesus, crying with a loud voice, said, "Father, into your hands I commend my spirit." Having said this, he breathed his last.

The title of this sermon is inspired by the book *Hope in the Holler*, written by womanist theologian A. Elaine Brown Crawford.[1] The book is a discourse on black women's understanding of God and our gift for being able to survive and endure despite **34** the multidimensional oppressions of racism, classism, and sexism. Crawford articulates how, through a theology of hope, black women are able to move beyond mere endurance and survival to transformation of these oppressive realities for our communities and ourselves. One of the keeping forces she says is our ability to "holler."

As I meditated on today's Scripture, I couldn't help but notice the similarities between Jesus' cry and Crawford's holler. I kept pondering this Scripture…Jesus called out "with a loud voice." Jesus *shouted*—wow! There is something in that. Jesus shouting…Lord, what could this mean? I began to imagine his loud cry. What was it like? Was it shrill? Was it agonized? Was it strong? Did it have some bass in it? Given the circumstances of crucifixion, I imagine it was an exhausted, labored shout, one that was so necessary, so important that it required every ounce of his remaining energy and power.

Some scholars suggest that this Scripture is tantamount to Jesus' serene acceptance of his fate. They go on to say that Jesus does not thrash about or exemplify anger or doubt as he enters the throes of death. I agree that Jesus does not seem to exhibit anger or doubt; however, I take issue with the notion that Jesus isn't wrestling with his death. While spiritually, he may have accepted this unjust punishment, I am hard pressed to believe that physically and emotionally he was not laboring in this situation. "What do you mean, Preacher?" Well, Jesus experienced hours of torture and torment, beatings and cursing; he was humiliated by the task of carrying his own instrument of death, and

Malene S. Minor is a Master of Divinity student at McCormick Theological Seminary in Chicago, Illinois. She is a licensed minister-in-training at Third Baptist Church of Chicago.

then he was subjected to the cruel and barbaric fate of crucifixion, suffering upon the Holy Rood. So desperate was Jesus to avoid this pain that he had prayed only hours earlier that his Father would take away this cup. His prayer was so intense that sweat poured from his body as though it were blood. Jesus' death on the cross is anything but serene.

I contend—watch this—that Jesus' divinity did not protect him from his humanity. Shall I make it plain? Though Jesus was fully divine, his divine nature was never meant to shield him from the human experiences of pain, sadness, frustration, disappointment, and every other emotion common to the human condition. Thus, Jesus felt the emotional pain of abandonment and the physical pain of being tortured and nailed to a cross.

The text declares that Jesus cried with a loud voice. His tone was not normal, nor did he whisper or mumble. Jesus hollered! "Father, into your hands, I commit my spirit."

You see to holler is to cry out in pain or protest. It comes from the word *hollo*, which is "to shout aloud; to incite or provoke." It is "to shout to or at something or someone." In his holler, Jesus was instigating the power of his relationship with Abba, his Father. Jesus was appealing to the only one who had the ability and responsibility to save.

Let me explain. When a father loves his child, he will do anything for that child. I watch my younger brother and his daughter. They have a special bond. Nothing and no one can come between them. She can count on him whenever she calls upon him. She knows that when she hollers for her daddy, he will respond. Jesus hollered for the one that he knew was well pleased with him when he was baptized. Jesus hollered for the one that he prayed to when he needed conversation, comfort, and renewal. He hollered for the one who spoke to him when he was

on the mountain called the Mount of Transfiguration. Jesus hollered, "Daddy!"

Now that we understand the holler, where is the hope? How can there be hope in such a painful holler? Where is the hope when Emmanuel, God with us, has been rejected? What of hope when the one sent to save the world is disregarded by the world? How can there be any hope when a man is falsely accused and convicted of a crime? Where is the hope when the Son of God is nailed to a cross, suffering an inhumane and anything-but-divine death? Where's the hope in his holler? I declare on this day that Jesus' holler had hope, because three elements were present: knowledge, experience, and relationship.

First, let us be clear that hope is not wishful thinking. You see, a wish is a longing or craving for something. A wish is merely a dream with no real expectation that it can come true. It is inactive and passive thinking. Inherent in a wish is hidden fear, with no basis in truth.

Ahh, but hope! Hope begins in truth because it begins in God. It requires something of you. Hope requires you to be confident in God. Hope requires you to trust God. Hope is your desire combined with expectation. It is the confident expectation of good in the future. Hope is based on the truth of who God is and has been. Hope is based on what God has done in the past and can or will do in the future.

Now that we understand holler and hope, how do relationship, knowledge, and experience combine to stir up this hope? When Jesus cried out, he did more than shout. He called on his Father. In his holler of hope, Jesus was crying, "It hurts, Daddy, but I trust you! I'm thirsty, Daddy, but living water is in you! Daddy, they are so mean to me, but I know you love me. I feel alone, Daddy, but I know you are with me! Daddy, they cursed me, but I know you have blessed me! Daddy, they have vilified me, but in you I'm glorified! I'm dying, Daddy, but I know you will raise me from the dead! But still…Daaadddy!"

When you call on Daddy, you're calling on the one with the wisdom, strength, skill, and power to change your circumstances. When you call Daddy, it's because you want the job to get done.

When Jesus hollered for his Father, he didn't holler just any ol' thing. Jesus hollered out Scripture! Jesus turned to the lessons of his youth. You know, the ancient version of Vacation Bible School, Sunday school, and Bible study. He remembered what he had been taught! All that temple training wasn't wasted!

Jesus reached back down the Davidic line, and he recalled what his ancestor King David had said when he was in trouble. Jesus' holler wasn't just loud talking; it was a prayer! It was a prayer of covering. Like King David, Jesus stood on the assurance of God's power and authority. He pulled up Psalm 31:5: "Into your hand, I commit my spirit"! If you expect this thing to work, you need to *know* something about the one on whom you call for help.

Jesus' holler had hope not only because of his relationship with the Father and his knowledge and appropriate application of Scripture, but he recalled his own experience of and with the Father. He recalled the experience of assisting his Father in turning chaos into creation. He remembered the glory they shared in heaven before the Father sent him to earth. Jesus recalled his transfiguration on that holy mountain. Jesus could reminisce over his experiences with his Father, and he knew what his Father was capable of.

You see, Jesus understood the purpose and mission for which his Father had sent him to earth. Jesus knew his mission would cause him to suffer, but knowing and living are two different things. It is the difference between knowledge and experience. Let me clarify. It

is like our near and distant kin, those who faced water hoses and dogs as they struggled to be treated as children of the Creator God, worthy of the same human and civil rights that God's fairer skinned children enjoy. God's left-out and left-behind children had been prepped in meetings and workshops on how to nonviolently resist the brutalities of racism. But being told how to resist evil and resisting evil are very different. It is a question of whether or not one will walk the talk. Jesus chose to move the knowledge of his mission and earthly purpose to the level of ultimate experience, death on a cross.

Life is what it is. If it hasn't made you holler yet…keep living! There are going to be some painstaking, cross-bearing, agonizing situations in your life! There will be some things that will leave you feeling betrayed, judged and misjudged, mocked, abused, and forsaken. I recall in my own life being questioned and challenged about the degree to which I would follow God's call into the ministry. How dare I give up a cushy job with salary, insurance benefits, and other perks? Those days made me holler. But then I remembered Jesus! I decided to do as Jesus did. I hollered for Abba Father, the one who promised never to leave or forsake me. I hollered with the promises of God in my heart and the Word on my lips! I hollered for the one who said he would supply all my needs according to his riches in glory. I hollered with the surety of God's presence, grace, and mercy! There was hope in my holler! And I stopped by to tell you what I learned a long time ago: Hope is what you hold on to until help shows up! If all you have is a holler and hope, then keep on because help is on the way! ✥

NOTE
1. A. Elaine Brown Crawford. *Hope in the Holler: A Womanist Theology* (Louisville: Westminster John Knox Press, 2002).

Join

a theological conversation between

the texts of faith
and the
people of faith

Go to www.ptsem.edu to explore the Princeton Seminary experience,
or come to one of our exploratory weekends.

October 12-15, 2006
November 9-12, 2006
November 30-December 3, 2006
February 1-4, 2007
February 15-18, 2007

PRINCETON
THEOLOGICAL SEMINARY

www.ptsem.edu
1.800.622.6767, ext. 1940

PRICELESS

REGINALD BELL JR.

Psalm 139:1-14, KJV

I will praise thee; for I am fearfully and wonderfully made; marvelous are thy works; and that my soul knoweth right well. (Psalm 139:14)

Tuxedo rental: $295. Floral arrangements: $2,800. Three-tier Bavarian chocolate wedding cake: $1,700. Photographer: $2,018. The grand total cost of my sister's

wedding: $11,000. The glow on her face as she walked down the aisle to take the hand of her beloved: priceless!

Many of us have seen the MasterCard commercial that reminds us that many material things have a price tag, but there are some things that money can't buy. The sentimental value of some things far exceeds monetary perimeters. If the head of the World Bank tried to write a check for some things, the check would come back marked "insufficient funds." Some things are so precious, so unique, so life-changing that it is impossible to attach a price tag that reflects the totality of their value. Such things are priceless.

For example, the cost of receiving counsel from a wise elder, that's priceless. To hear a loved one say, "I admire you and I love you," that's priceless. And the privilege of being able to get on your knees each night and pray to a God who says, "Ask and it shall be given…," that's priceless!

There is something else in this world that's priceless, but many of us fail to fathom its value. But what is it? You see it every day. It goes wherever you go. It has been with you for as long as you have existed. What is this priceless phenomenon? It's *you!*

The text before us is taken from the One-hundred Thirty-ninth Psalm. It is called an individual psalm. Unlike most psalms, this one was not created to be recited in corporate worship by the whole Israelite community. Rather this psalm was designed for the individual worshiper. In Jewish antiquity, there were times when the whole community worshiped God together, and everyone quoted

Reginald Bell Jr. is a Master of Divinity student at Candler School of Theology at Emory University in Atlanta, Georgia.

the same psalm. But then there were times when individuals would go to the temple, find a psalm that spoke to their personal situation, and then recite it to God as if it were their own words. I imagine this particular psalm would have been quoted by someone who needed their self-esteem increased. For example, this psalm would have helped Job after he lost everything: children, health, friends, home, animals, everything. This psalm would have been valuable to Tamar who, as a woman without means, felt that she had to act as a prostitute to receive justice.

Just as this psalm was a valuable resource in biblical times, I believe it has relevance today. Just as it was recited then, I believe it needs to be recited today. It needs to be read by people who on the outside appear to have it all together, but if we could get a glimpse into their mind for a moment, we would see that the outward appearance is very deceptive. If we could hear the conversations in their conscience, we would hear a small voice inside crying out for help. They're singing like Smokey Robinson: "Now, if there's a smile on my face, it's only there to fool the public; now when it comes down to how I really feel, now honey that's quite a different subject."[1]

This psalm needs be recited by the countless number of people who hate what they see in the mirror. By the countless number of women who are physically, emotionally, and verbally abused daily. It needs to be read by those contemplating suicide. It needs to be read by men and women who look for life's happiness in bottles, babes, and Benjamins. It needs to be read by everyone who does not know who they are. But why? Well, let me show you.

Psalm 139 begins with the psalmist informing us of who God is. Before he puts the magnifying glass or the spotlight on himself, the writer shines the light on God. In verses 1-5,

the psalmist acknowledges God's omniscience—his God knows all about him! In verse 6 the psalmist says that God's ways are not our ways and are just too deep for us to understand. In verses 7-10, the psalmist describes God as omnipresent; God is in all things and present everywhere.

I like the way this psalm is tailored because before the psalmist looked at himself, he acknowledged God. Before he attempts to explain himself, he decides to talk about his God, to reflect upon his Creator. Before he views himself in the mirror of personal reflection or self image, he shows off his God. Then he steps up behind God and observes himself through the loving, transforming eyes of God. See, if you can see yourself through the eyes of God, then you can get a clear picture, a complete picture, and a correct picture.

As he looks at himself through the eyes of God, in verse 13 the psalmist asserts, "For you did form my inward parts; you did knit me together in my mother's womb." Right there the psalmist is saying, "I am not an accident. My birth was divinely planned. I know I am somebody because God doesn't make junk. Every single part of my body has God's stamp of approval on it." Then in verse 14 he concludes, "I am fearfully and wonderfully made." That's the first thing I'd like you to remember today: You are priceless because God made you.

As I contemplated the fact that God made me, I was able to conceive a mental image of how it happened. With my spiritual imagination, I could see God as a divine architect. Then God had a conversation with God and said: "I think I'll sit down and design myself a Reginald Bell Jr." Then God began to sketch out my body. God said, "I think I'll make him a black man with a lot of protective melanin in his skin. I'll give him small ears, brown eyes, a midsize nose, and a mole right above his full

**If you can see yourself through the eyes of God,
then you can get a clear picture, a complete picture,
and a correct picture.**

lips. I think I'll give him kinky hair—since I make all hair, it's all good. I'll give him a thick neck, broad shoulders, some flat feet, and some sexy legs. (I have some sexy legs, ya'll!) I will also give him some charisma and a thirst for knowledge, a big heart and the anointing to preach my Word."

After God finished designing me, God rolled up the blueprints and placed them in a case labeled RBJ 1981, Birmingham, Alabama. Next, God took off his architect's hat and put on a construction hat. Then God walked out of the Royal Room, peered down over the balcony of heaven, and tossed a seed into the universe. And when my mother's cycle didn't come that month, it was God's way of saying, "This area is under construction."

And for the next nine months, like a potter with clay in skilled hands, God shaped, God molded every inch, every piece of my body. God tailor made me the way God wanted me to be. And when God finished, I came forth as the epitome of God's creative imagination.

Because God made me, I am fearfully and wonderfully made. I agree with the psalmist on that. But what do the words *fearfully* and *wonderfully* really mean? In Hebrew these two words have the same meaning. First, both mean "to cause astonishment and awe, to stand in awe of." Simply put, because God made you, people should be astonished and stand in awe every time they see you. Hearts should stop whenever you enter a room. Mouths should drop and eyes should buck every time your presence is manifested because you are one of a kind.

No one else has what you have or can do what you can do.

Fearfully and *wonderfully* also mean "respectfully." You deserve respect simply because God made you. You deserve to be treated with honor and respect. Because God made you, when you speak, people should listen to what you have to say. No one should ever talk to you like you're less than human. No one has any business putting their hands on you. You may not be Halle Berry or Denzel Washington, but because God made you, you still deserve respect. You may not be Aretha Franklin, but you still deserve respect!

I was in Paris, France, a few years ago. One of the places I visited was the Louvre. Inside of the Louvre was the priceless painting, the *Mona Lisa*. Prior to entering the gallery, I was given instructions on what I could and could not do. Upon entering the room, I noticed that everyone inside stood in awe and astonishment. Furthermore, I noticed that not only was the *Mona Lisa* behind several inches of thick glass, but it was barricaded. No one could get within five feet of it, and there were police officers all over the room. Now, if Leonardo da Vinci can create a painting that demands awe and respect, then anything made by the One who created da Vinci deserves nothing less! God created you, so you are fearfully and wonderfully made—priceless.

The next thing that this text shows us is that the cosmos is a testimony of how priceless you are. The psalmist says, "I am fearfully and wonderfully made; marvelous are thy works." This statement has two implications.

First, he reaffirms the fact that he is special. "Marvelous are thy works." Since I was made by God, I am marvelous.

However, his next statement goes into broader territory than himself. "Marvelous are thy *works*." Marvelous are thy *works*. Notice, *works* is plural. This statement alludes to everything that God has made and will ever make. This statement covers so much territory that it reaches all the way back to the Creation story in Genesis 1. It reaches back to when God smiled and the light broke, and the darkness receded. It stretches back to when God reached out and took the light in his hands and rolled the light around until he fashioned the sun and then took what was left and made the moon. It includes when God walked and as he walked his footsteps hollowed out the valleys and bulged up the mountains. It reaches back to when the green grass sprouted, little red flowers blossomed, pine trees pointed their fingers to the sky, the oak spread out its arms, and the rivers ran down to the sea. It goes back to when God said to the land and sea, "Bring forth, bring forth. And fish and fowl, beasts and birds, jumped into the rivers and the seas, and roamed the forests and the woods, and split the air with their wings."[2] The statement, "Marvelous are thy works" pays homage the creation of the cosmos.

As I pondered the phenomenon of creation, it dawned on me that God created these marvelous things for us. Because God wanted the cosmos to be inhabited, God created man and woman. After God made man and woman, God said, "Be fruitful and multiply…have dominion over…every living thing that moveth upon the earth."[3] Then God said to humanity, "I have given you every herb-bearing seed…and every tree, and every beast…, and every fowl, and every-thing that creepeth."[4] God said, "I give it all to you!"

The psalmist said, "Marvelous are thy works." God said, "I give it all to you." What I am saying is that because God thinks so highly of you, because you are so priceless, the cosmos in all its greatness, splendor, and beauty, is God's testimony of how much God thinks of you. The cosmos is the manifested expression of God's admiration for humanity.

I used to be very shy when it came to talking to girls. When I was in the tenth grade, I really liked this girl, but she didn't know it. To be honest she really didn't know I existed. I had seen her in the halls one day, and I just started liking her. Since I could not find the words to express to her how I felt, she did not understand the feelings I had. Because Valentine's Day was approaching, I decided to get her a nice teddy bear and a card. On Valentine's Day, I got one of her friends to slip the gift in her locker. When the girl got the gift, although I could not explain to her how I felt, the gift in her locker with my name on it told my story.

I share that to say this: because God is so completely other, it is hard for us to comprehend how God feels about us. But I am glad to know that God has given us an infinite number of clues to show how God feels. Therefore, the next time you look up at a captivating cloud, know that that's God's way of saying, "You're priceless." The next time you see a sensational sunrise, that's God's way of saying, "You are priceless." The next time that you see the marvelous moonlight, know that that's God's way of saying, "You are priceless." The next time that you observe a red, riveting rose or hear a bird's serenade, know that that's God's way of saying, "You are priceless."

The last thing this text teaches us is that you are priceless because of what's on the inside of you. The psalmist said, "My soul knoweth it well." The Hebrew word for "soul" is *nephesh*; it refers to the inner being of a person. It is the true you. The soul is the safe deposit box in which God houses our purpose, destiny, and mission.

The psalmist said, "My soul knoweth it well." My soul—my inner self, the emotions inside of me, my sixth sense—knows that I am fearfully and wonderfully made because it knows what God has deposited inside of it. Because my soul houses a divine purpose, that makes me priceless.

A few years ago I went to the store and bought a young lady a very expensive six-disc CD changer for her car. After I bought the gift, I took it to a department store to have it wrapped. In an effort to impress the girl, I chose very expensive wrapping paper, I got a nice ribbon, and I chose a fancy ornament. When I gave her the gift, she looked at the box and said, "Oh, it's beautiful." However, she then removed the ornament, she removed the ribbon, and she removed the wrapping paper because she understood the most important, the most valuable part of the gift was not on the outside of the container—it was on the inside! Lord, have mercy.

Behind your Fashion Fair makeup, your weaved or faded-cut hairstyle, or your Italian suit or shoes is a priceless soul that houses the ability to make an eternal difference.

Let me show you. Inside of Moses was a set of directions to the Promised Land. Inside of Paul were the churches of Corinth, Rome, Galatia, and more. Inside of you is a poem that only you can write. Inside of you is a song that only you can sing. Inside of you is a purpose that only you can achieve. Inside of you is justice that only you can bring.

As I conclude, I want to invite you to ponder a few questions. The first set of questions begins with "How long?" How long will you

continue to hate yourself? How long will you have low self-esteem? How long will you contemplate suicide? How long will you stay in that abusive relationship? How long will you keep allowing people to disrespect you?

The next set of questions begin with "When?" When will you become aware of whose you are, from whom you came, and to whom you are headed? When will you recognize that God made you? When will you start looking at yourself through the loving, transformative eyes of God? When will you accept that you are priceless?

When? When Jacob realized how priceless he was, he ran into an angel one night and said, "I am so priceless, I am not going to let you go until you bless me."[5] When Mary the mother of Jesus realized how priceless she was, she said "My soul doth magnify the Lord."[6] When Maya Angelou realized how priceless she was, she said: "I am a phenomenal woman."[7] When Nelly realized how priceless he was, he said "I am number one."[8] When James Brown realized how priceless he was, he said, "Say it loud, I'm black and I am proud."[9]

When! When I think of the goodness of God and all he has done for me, my soul cries out hallelujah. The psalmist had a praise on his lips because he knew he was priceless! ❖

NOTES
1. From "Tears of a Clown," lyrics by Smokey Robinson and The Miracles, Make It Happen. Motown Records, 1968.
2. James Weldon Johnson, "The Creation" (In *God's Trombones: Seven Negro Sermons in Verse*), 1927.
3. Genesis 1:28.
4. Genesis 1:29-30.
5. See Genesis 32:26.
6. Luke 1:46.
7. Maya Angelou. *Phenomenal Woman: Four Poems Celebrating Women* (Random House, 1995), 3–6.
8. "Number 1," words by Nelly, Nellyville. Umvd Labels, 2002.
9. "Say It Loud: I'm Black and I'm Proud," words by James Brown and Alfred "Pee-Wee" Ellis. Universal Records, 1968.

Tell me again:
What is worship really all about?

CALVIN SYMPOSIUM ON WORSHIP

Grand Rapids, Michigan, USA, January 25-27, 2007

- Over 70 workshops and several day-long seminars on every aspect of public worship

- Worship planners, pastors, musicians, artists, scholars and worshipers in dialogue

- Attendees from 30 denominations and 10 countries

- Featured sessions on preaching sponsored by the Center for Excellence in Preaching at Calvin Theological Seminary (see *http://cep.calvinseminary.edu*)

- Over 50 presenters including Carol Bechtel, Horace Boyer, Ellen Davis, Keith & Kristyn Getty, Pedrito Maynard-Reid, Hughes Oliphant Old, Stephen Breck Reid, and Pablo Sosa

- Registration and program information on the web

CALVIN INSTITUTE OF CHRISTIAN WORSHIP   *www.calvin.edu/worship*

The Ministry of LIBERATION: A Call and Response

D. DARIUS BUTLER

Exodus 3:3-5, NIV

Then Moses said, "I must turn aside and look at this great sight, and see why the bush is not burned up." When the LORD saw that he had turned aside to see, God called to him out of the bush, "Moses, Moses!" And he said, "Here I am." Then he said, "Come no closer! Remove the sandals from your feet, for the place on which you are standing is holy ground."

"Lord, bless Dkcruma…keep Desmond… protect Devon…sustain Robert… watch over Don." This was the cry of a faithful single-parent mother, who rose early every morning to petition her God and to intercede for her children. Under the bondage of poverty and substandard living conditions, amid family advice for her to offer her children for adoption, and even in the presence of a God who seemed silent, she prayed—religiously she prayed. This is the witness of my mother.

In recalling such a precious testimony, I remember being awakened by her prayers— her whimpering but resolute voice—calling on the God in whom she believed for help in raising and providing for her children; for strength to withstand criticism, even from her family; and for integrity, to set a good example. While my brothers, all older than I, enjoyed the last of their sleep, as the morning broke through the darkness, I never could return to a posture of slumber because my heart would become heavy: my mother was crying—praying, yet crying.

Sometimes I went where she was and touched her; other times, I watched from a distance. Whether near or far, my heart wrenched with hers. Every time she prayed I would ask, "Where is God? Why hasn't God responded? Does God not hear her prayer?" There was no response to these urgent questions, and I was left to bear them in my own soul. But today, this text offers answers to those questions I raised.

The drama unfolds beyond the wilderness, on the rocky ridges of Mount Horeb, when Moses is interrupted by God. An urgent call comes—a call that draws on the sensory perceptions of Moses. An angel of the Lord appears; a bush blazes but isn't consumed; a voice calls from the bush: "Moses, Moses." A command is spoken: "Come no closer, remove the sandals from your feet, feel mother earth, for the place on which you are standing is holy ground."

D. Darius Butler is a Kelly Miller Smith Scholar at Vanderbilt University Divinity School in Nashville, Tennessee, where he is pursuing a Master of Divinity degree.

While the writer begins this narrative with Moses, permit me to posit that it really begins with the children of Israel, who cry out to God. Their desperate plea for deliverance is the first call. Their call arrests God's attention and demands a response. God's response to their cry becomes another call. And that is the call to which Moses and every minister must respond.

The language of the text, particularly the language of God, is most compelling: "I have observed the misery of my people…I have heard their cry…I know their sufferings…I have come down to deliver them…" Not only does God hear their cry, but God is concerned—concerned enough to break into human history on their behalf. It is the tradition of call and response.

The cry of the human family moves God to respond, and God's response to humanity's cry is liberation. But the way God brings about liberation is worth exploring. Essentially, that is what this text fleshes out. From this narrative we can deduce that the ministry of liberation involves a divine-human partnership; it involves the joining of our witness with God's plan for human freedom.

The call which comes to Moses does not end with Moses; it continues. It compels us— yes, us as divinity students—to be agents of liberation, setting the captives free. It is the call that has brought us here, and it is the same call that will take us from here to our respective assignments in a world of oppression and bondage.

Whatever we take from this text, we cannot deny that the author purposefully intends to highlight God's preferential option for those who are oppressed, those who are in bondage, and those who are exploited. It is that preferential option for the oppressed that begins the ministry to which God calls our gifts, our talents, our empathy, our expertise,

our experience, our training, and our actions. God says to us through Moses, "I am sending you to 'Pharaoh' to deliver my people from bondage, to release them from the indignity of suffering, to restore their sense of worth, and to proclaim to them their great potential." What an awesome task! God's use of us to do such important work is overwhelming.

But just as it is with Moses, it is with us. We too have reservations, feelings of uncertainty, second thoughts. I would be the first to admit that it sounds good—"agents of liberation," "stewards of human freedom," "ministers of the oppressed." But I just don't know if I can do it. I don't know if I can face the powers; I don't know if I can be the one to speak the right words; I wouldn't know where to begin; I don't know if I have the right credentials.

What about my past? What about what I did? What about the place from where I came? God's reply is: "I can use it; just go. I can use your uncertainty; I can use your fear; I can use your failures; I can use your story. Just go! I can use them all in ministry; just go and set the captives free." But when you go, know that you are not alone! God declares, "I will be with you…" That's good news! The task may be great, but the one who goes with us is greater!

The assurance of God's presence in ministry is most important, especially as it is revealed in this text. Moses begs of God to give him a name that will resonate with the children of Israel: "Who shall I say has sent me?" Possessing a name under which to march implies authority. It suggests that I am not acting on my behalf, but on behalf of another, one who is greater than I am. When my mother would send me on an errand to ask something of a relative, she would always preface the instructions: "Tell them that *I* said…" If when I arrived, I did not use the same preface as my mother, I would not be heard and my request would go unfulfilled. But when I used those words, "*My mother said…*" it would yield a different response.

God's response to Moses, "I AM WHO I AM," indicates that God's authority would also be there with God's presence. The revelation of this name in verb form connotes that our reference to God should never be that of a God who is still and passive, but rather a God who is present and active—active in our ministries. That presence enables us to engage in the ministry of liberation.

God's abiding presence sustains us when we confront and dismantle racism and affirm that all people are fashioned in God's image. God's abiding presence protects us when we shatter the glass ceiling of sexism, declaring that women, too, are first-class citizens in the commonwealth of God. God's abiding presence prompts us to address the unequal distribution of wealth, while calling for the sharing of the world's resources. God's abiding presence urges us to speak for love—yes, love—that cord that binds together all human relationships. And it was God's abiding presence that became my compassion when I heard my mother pray; I just could not claim it then.

The beauty of this text is the clear claim that God uses people to bring about liberation. The text witnesses to God's desire to enter the magnificence and mess of the human condition with and through us. When God says, "Go down Moses…" God is not sending him; God is asking him to be a vessel through which God will do God's bidding. And when God calls us, God is asking us to do and to be the same.

An infinite God uses people—finite people, frail people, fractured people—to bring about liberation. If we are willing, God is more than able to use us in mighty ways to do mighty works. God is still saying, "Go down, Moses,

and set my people free…free from the bondage of addiction…free from the burden of self-hatred…free from the choke-hold of poverty…"

Go down, Moses, and set them free…free from the spirit of hopelessness…free from the misery of discrimination…free from the agony of abandonment. Set them free…free from the stereotypes that say they will never be good enough…free from a reality that robs them of their dignity…free from circumstances that strip them of their humanity…Set them free!

And there is more to God's divine imperative upon us. God says further, "When you set them free, bring them up to a good land. Bring them up to good land and give them something to live for. Bring them up to a good land and give them a hope for the future. Bring them up to a good land and proclaim to them their great potential. Bring them up to a good land and declare to them my purposes."

Bring them up to a good land and welcome them into a community that will include them regardless of where they were born. Bring them up to a good land and love them in spite of their past addictions. Bring them up to a good land and provide for them a place of rehabilitation. Bring them up to a good land and secure healing for the uninsured. Bring them up to a good land and restore the dignity of those living in despair. Bring them up to a good land and rekindle hope in those whose candles have gone out. Bring them up to a good land and provide restoration to those who have fallen. Bring them to the place where they can live as I intended them to live: free…free…free! "Go down, Moses, way down in Egypt's land, tell ol' Pharaoh, let my people go!"[1] ❖

NOTE

1. "Go Down Moses (Let My People Go)," Negro spiritual, public domain.

ENDING the Identity Crisis: Do You KNOW HIM?

LISA M. GOODS

Matthew 16:13-15, NIV

Now when Jesus came into the district of Caesarea Philippi, he asked his disciples, "Who do people say that the Son of Man is?" And they said, "Some say John the Baptist, but others Elijah, and still others Jeremiah or

one of the prophets." He said to them, "But who do you say that I am?"

In society today one of the psychological or sociological terms we all seem to have become familiar with is *identity crisis*, which Webster defines as "the state of being uncertain about oneself regarding character, goals, etc." And I believe it is that *etcetera* that catches us all. At one time or another we all seem to have suffered from an identity crisis. Like most people we are trying to find ourselves—concerned with the image we portray, what people think of us, and unfortunately, sometimes more concerned with what others think than we are with what *God* thinks. Everyone seems to be seeking his or her destiny, trying to live that "purpose-driven life." In fact, we have whole communities and generations in identity crisis. Many of our black leaders, sociologists, historians, and educators tell us that the African American community as a whole is going through an identity crisis. The dismantling of our communities through desegregation, despite some good that it did, seems to have left us in a state of cultural amnesia. We have no unified agenda. No collective goals. No mutual identity. Gentrification and assimilation have scattered us so that we are facing an identity crisis!

And if I were to be honest with you, I myself just a few short months ago, having turned 40, found myself in a sort of identity crisis. I was wondering what life would be like from now on. Had I reached all of my goals? In fact, what are my goals? Was I even the same

Lisa M. Goods is Master of Divinity Student at McCormick Theological Seminary in Chicago, Illinois.

person? Society, the media, and all the hype had told me something magical was supposed to happen at age 40, so I began to question life myself. This is not exactly bad. I believe we all need to do that from time to time—examine our lives to find our true identity, but it does not necessarily have to be a crisis.

I believe this text gives us the means to end our collective and individual identity crisis. Here we have Jesus and the twelve disciples on the coast of Caesarea Philippi. Up to this point Jesus had healed the sick, cleansed lepers, calmed the raging seas, cast out demons, caused the lame to walk, unstopped deaf ears, brought the dead to life, fed the multitudes, and walked on water, and yet it seems people still didn't understand who Jesus was. In fact chapters 11–16 in Matthew are dedicated to giving people an opportunity to discern Jesus' true identity. Then at the beginning of chapter 16, the Pharisees and Sadducees, who don't even like each other, get together in an effort to entrap Jesus and ask him for a sign. A sign as to whether he was the Messiah, the king of the Jews, the prophesied coming king. Jesus, having refused to reveal to them a sign, now questioned his disciples, "Who do people say that the Son of Man is?"

It might seem at first glance that Jesus is going through a sort of identity crisis, trying to figure out what people were saying about him. But when you look at the text, you see that Jesus clearly identified himself as the Son of Man…This was a set up! Jesus always knew who he was, is, and shall be! He also didn't really care what people thought of him. He was giving the disciples the opportunity to acknowledge who he was. Even today Jesus is constantly setting up opportunities for us to acknowledge who he is. The problem is we are so consumed with ourselves, our situations, our problems, that we forget about the fish and the loaves, the walking on water, the

healings, how he made a way out of no way. But even when we forget, ain't it just like God to send us a reminder—like how he stretched that paycheck or put that $20 in a coat pocket for you to find when you didn't have bus fare or your child needed lunch money. Or how he got us that degree and that job when they told us we wouldn't amount to anything. We get so busy looking at people and circumstances that we forget to acknowledge who Jesus is. But is there anybody here honest enough to admit that even when I have forgotten to acknowledge Jesus, he always sends a faithful reminder? My God!

So he asks them, "Who do people say the Son of Man is?" And so the disciples (being his road dogs and, I believe, not wanting to hurt his feelings) give him the politically correct answer: "Some say John the Baptist, but others Elijah and still others Jeremiah or one of the prophets." These answers were true, for the record is that people had speculated that Jesus might be all of these. But among the rulers and leaders, he had also been compared to Beelzebub and called a blasphemer.

Then of course there were those who couldn't get past his past. You know the ones. You'd hear them on the streets or in the market saying, "Oh, that's just Jesus—you know Mary and Joseph's boy, the carpenter's son. Girl, he from Nazareth. You know don't nothing good come out of Nazareth." They couldn't see past his beginning to see who God created him to be. And even today in 2006 right here, there are those who would question our true identity. There are those who can't see past our pasts. There are those who don't recognize the God in us. And so Jesus asks, "Who do people say I am?"

Upon hearing their answer, Jesus redirects his question to the Twelve—his disciples, those who had been closest to him. You see, the people had seen *some* of the miracles and heard about others, but the Twelve had been with him from the beginning. They were *on* the boat when the storms were raging, and he said, "Peace be still." They *passed out* the seven loaves and the few small fish to the four thousand, and they *collected* the seven baskets of leftovers. They were *there*. They witnessed the healings and deliverances. They had seen each one of them. So he asked them, "After all that you have seen, heard, and felt, who do *you* say that I am?" And if I were to go back to my old Baptist church testimony service roots, I would say that after all that they had witnessed, they should have been "poppin up like popcorn" to answer Jesus' question! Yet it was only Peter who spoke up, saying, "You are the Messiah, the Son of the living God."

If you know anything about Peter, you know he didn't do anything half-heartedly. He was outspoken and confident. I believe Peter said to himself, "Jesus, I know who you are. I watched you heal all those people. I watched you raise the lame and give sight to the blind. I watched you stand for the homeless and victimized. It was you, Jesus, who healed my mother-in-law when the family was losing hope. But even more than that, it was you who took me from casting a net to catch a few measly fish to walking on the water with power and authority. And even when I took my eye off of you and began to sink, it was you, Jesus, who caught me with your hand of love. Oh yeah, I know who you are. You are the Messiah! Son of the Living God!"

Is there anybody in here who knows what I'm talking about? Is there anybody who has watched Jesus work in their lives? Is there anybody who has watched him raise family members off their sick beds? Is there anybody who has been crippled by some habit, some addiction, some relationship, and Jesus gave you the power to rise up and walk? Ask your neighbor, "Do you know him?"

You see, Peter had an intimate personal relationship with God. That is why he could say without a doubt, "You are the Messiah, Son of the living God." That is the kind of relationship that comes only through worship. And through that relationship, he was open enough in his spirit to see the God in Jesus. That's why Jesus tells him, "Flesh and blood didn't reveal this to you, but my Father in heaven."

And it is right here that Jesus does something. All this time he has been talking about who people said he was and now what does he do? He flips the script. He says, "And I tell you, you are Peter, and on this rock I will build my church and the gates of Hades will not prevail against it."

He goes from who he is to who Peter is. Ain't that just like Jesus to flip the script? Because once you know who Jesus is, he can begin to tell you who you are! I'm talking about the intimate personal relationship kind of knowledge, where Jesus is the lover of your soul.

So he says, "You are Peter." You see, when Jesus called Peter to discipleship, he said, "You *shall* be called" Peter. He was foretelling Peter's new identity, but the name wasn't actually bestowed upon him until now. Now he was no longer Simon—Simon the fisherman, Simon the uneducated. He was Peter! Why? Because Jesus knew what Peter was going to have to face. You see, Jesus was not just changing Simon's name, but Jesus was also revealing his destiny. Jesus said, "You are Peter, and on this rock I will build my church." This was a foretelling of his coming role. *Peter*, meaning rock. *Rock*, meaning a foundation. Look at Isaiah 28:16 where it says God lays "a foundation…a tested stone," a precious cornerstone, and a name is inscribed on it: "He who has faith shall not waver." Peter didn't waver. Jesus is foretelling Peter's destiny as a foundation of the church.

Jesus knew Peter would have some obstacles to overcome. Peter was going to be the one preaching and teaching these people, and he was a Galilean. Galileans spoke funny and had trouble pronouncing certain sounds. It was something like having a Mississippi accent in Chicago. You know how people can be. I can hear them talking right now. "Who does he think he is, comin' up in here with his old country self, trying to tell somebody about Jesus? My family built this synagogue. Wasn't he the one who denied Jesus at the cross? You know he only walked on water for a minute anyway, and then Jesus had to get him up out of that water before he drowned." Jesus knew what Peter would have to face. Jesus knew Peter had to be confident in who he was. He couldn't have an identity crisis, so Jesus changed his name. Jesus changed it from fisher to preacher, from denier to testifier, from stumbling block to "upon this rock." He changed Peter's name, and I believe somebody here needs a name change. You are not a single parent; you are a primary parent, a principle provider, a qualified care-giving queen or king. You are not an ex-con or an ex-offender; you are redeemed by the blood of the lamb. You are not an addict; you are delivered. You are not a refugee or a victim; you are a survivor! You are not a hoochie or a thug; you are a child of God, fearfully and wonderfully made. You are the head and not the tail. I don't know about you, but "I told Jesus it would be alright if he changed my name."[1]

When you know Jesus, you can walk in victory. Jesus says, "Upon this rock I will build my church, and the gates of Hell shall not prevail against it." When you know Jesus, you know who you are. When you know Jesus, you know what you are called to do. When you know Jesus, there is nothing that can stop you. When you realize your Jesus-identity, you know that if you don't have a dime in your pocket, the Lord will make a way somehow. When you realize your Jesus-identity, you know that no weapon that is formed against you shall prosper. When you realize your Jesus-identity, you know that you are more than a conqueror through him who loves you. You no longer have to sing my soul looks back and wonders, because you already know how you got over, even in the midst of your situation. When you know Jesus, you know that the way was already made for you more than two thousand years ago on a hill called Calvary. When you know Jesus, you know that he was wounded for your transgressions. When you know Jesus, you know he was bruised for your iniquity. When you know Jesus, you know that the chastisement of your peace was upon him. When you know Jesus, you know that by his stripes you are healed.

Do you know him? When you really find out who Jesus is, he will change your name. He will show you your destiny, and you can walk in victory. He will end the identity crisis in your life.

Stop trying to find yourself. Stop trying to find your identity. Stop trying to find your purpose. If you really want to end your identity crisis, find Jesus. The real Jesus! The Jesus who makes you say from the depths of your soul: "You are not only the Messiah, the Savior, the Son of the Living God, but you are *my* Messiah, *my* Savior, *my* Redeemer, *my* Deliverer, *my* Way-maker, *my* Friend." Find Jesus! The Word of God says, "Seek ye first the kingdom of God and his righteousness and all these things will be added unto you."[2] Do you know Jesus? ❖

NOTES

1. "Changed Mah Name," Negro spiritual. Public domain.
2. Matthew 6:33, KJV.

Worship...

sheer wonder at the beauty of God,
gratitude for the gospel of Christ,
and eagerness to deepen
self-giving service in God's world.

What new step of creativity, faithfulness, or congregational insight
would it take for your church to further pursue this ideal?
At the Calvin Institute of Christian Worship, we offer no easy
answers. But through our Worship Renewal Grants Program,
we do offer practical encouragement and financial support:

We seek to serve as a catalyst to **stimulate** and **implement** your
vision for worship with greater creativity, depth, and relevance.

We **encourage and guide** you as you develop a collaborative
plan for imaginative but well-grounded worship renewal.

We **listen** and **learn** from a diverse community of grant recipients.
Through seminars, correspondence, and our website, those who receive
Worship Renewal Grants exchange ideas and learn from one another.

Learn more at the Grants section of our website
www.calvin.edu/worship

CALVIN INSTITUTE OF CHRISTIAN WORSHIP
for the study and renewal of worship

Worship Renewal Grants Program:
To enrich public worship in your congregation.
Funding from Lilly Endowment Inc.

A GRAVE DANGER Disciples Face

TAFT QUINCEY HEATLEY

Matthew 3:1-12, NIV

But when he saw many of the Pharisees and Sadducees coming to where he was baptizing, he said to them: "You brood of vipers! Who warned you to flee from the coming wrath? Produce fruit in keeping with repentance. And do not think you can say to yourselves, 'We have Abraham as our father.' I tell you that out of these stones God can raise up children for Abraham. The ax is already at the root of the trees, and every tree that does not produce good fruit will be cut down and thrown into the fire." (Matthew 3:7-10)

There is a danger that looms large in the life of every disciple. It involves an interplay between perception and reality. On one hand

Taft Quincey Heatley is a 2007 candidate for a Master of Divinity at Princeton Theological Seminary. He is an associate minister at Emmanuel Baptist Church in Brooklyn, New York.

we perceive ourselves as the proper representatives of the kingdom of God who proclaim the Good News. We preach the power of the gospel that liberates the oppressed, comforts the distressed, and heals the wounded. As a result of this, we feel as if we matter because successful ministry can foster feelings of self-worth and self-satisfaction. But if our emotions regarding our success are not handled properly, they can manifest signs of superiority, elitism, and pompousness. In this reality we elevate ourselves above those to whom we minister. We stop acknowledging that our success is due to God and God alone. It becomes about us, not about the God who graces us. Here lies a grave danger—an arrogance that God abhors.

This interplay between perception and reality is present in the two dispositions of the characters of the text—John the Baptist and the Jewish religious elite. In Matthew 3:1-12 we find one in the desert of Judea known as John the Baptist, who gives a decree for all in his vicinity to "repent for the kingdom of heaven has come near."[1] Our text informs us that he is baptizing at the river Jordan. But verse 7 tells us that some uninvited guests have arrived. The Pharisees and Sadducees have come seeking baptism, but instead they are repudiated by the wilderness prophet who refers to them as a "brood of vipers." Instead, they are instructed to bear fruit worthy of repentance. The verbal exchange between John the Baptist and the Pharisees and Sadducees is symbolic of the psychological conflict that resides within the minds and hearts of each disciple—our perception of our position and the reality.

Our perception is that we are more like John the Baptist. We like to perceive ourselves as representatives of the kingdom of God. We affirm that God has gifted us to teach, preach, and minister to those far and near. But within our vocation is a specific purpose that God has ordained for us, just as God did for the preacher of our text. John the Baptist's purpose is to "prepare the way of Lord." He is the herald of the one who is to come. His announcement is a call to repentance and faith, and for this purpose he was created. He is the earthly facilitator of the ministry commencement of our Lord and Savior.

Analogous to John, you and I have been created for a purpose, and God shows faithfulness to us in its revelation. When we begin to function in our purpose, we will realize how God has gifted and wired us. Truly, God has done some amazing things in and through us. But we must always remember that it is *God* who enables and equips us, and not we ourselves. Failure to acknowledge the God who strengthens us to minister is what establishes an environment for arrogance. Haughty and lofty

notions about our callings cause us to create the wrong self-realities. In our work for the kingdom, we must heed the words of the apostle Paul who declared, "Do not think of yourself more highly than you ought, but rather think of yourselves with sober judgment."[2] If not, our reality will become like that of the Pharisees and Sadducees—those who exalt themselves because of their religious affiliations, but fail to offer authentic and true worship. Disciples, this is dangerous.

When our ministry, gifts, and talents become about us and not about our God, we lose sincerity and authenticity in our work. We become adept at functioning as Christians, and we become experts on how to be churched. But in all of our "churchness," our work is just not real. Our ministry is no more than a perfunctory practice that is void of an honest appreciation of God. And this was the disposition of the Pharisees and the Sadducees. They both possessed a formal pietism, but it was replete with insincerity. What they claimed as a zeal for their God was nothing more than a zeal for their traditions and status. This fake religiosity by the religious aristocracy is what Paul Tillich calls *hubris*, better known as puffed-up pride. When hubris seeps in and saturates us, we affirm ourselves by centering all of our thoughts on us and not on our Creator. Another unfortunate result is a selfishness that causes us to exalt our self-worth above those who dwell outside our respective circles—namely those to whom we should minister. Therefore we produce fruit that is unworthy of repentance.

What is the remedy for this malady? Instead of being drunk on the wine of our own self-importance, we should "bear fruit of repentance." The Greek word for repentance is

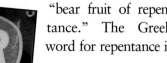

metanoia. It means "to change one's mind in a radical way." Bearing fruit worthy of *metanioa* should generate a conduct that is conducive to one whose mind has been radically changed.

This issue reminds me of a child who performed household chores solely for a weekly allowance. His only motivation for working was the allowance and not because he appreciated

his parents. Although he performed the chores when he did not receive an allowance, his heart was not in it. His work was not authentic. But one day his mind and heart were reoriented. He came to himself. He recognized the sacrifices that his mother and father continuously made for him. He began doing chores seeking nothing in return. He even performed without being asked to do so. He merely wanted to express his love and gratitude in any way that he could. This is fruit worthy of repentance—works done out of appreciation and love.

But how is this achieved? Humility prepares the heart for this type of ministry. Humility is where our hope exists and where the danger of poisonous pride is avoided. The way to avoid this danger is to remain humble throughout our ministry. Our constant acknowledgment of the power of God in our ministry keeps us humble. We remain humble when we realize that our mission is for the kingdom and not for our self promotion. And how is this humility presented in our text? Through the words of the prophet. In his humility, John the Baptist recognizes his place and acknowl-

edges that the one who is to come is more powerful that him. He admits that he is not even fit to carry that one's sandals. In humility, John understands that his mission is to proclaim the one who will baptize with the Holy Spirit and fire.

In such humility is where our hope exists. How is there hope? Because the one of whom John spoke has indeed come. There is hope because his ax is at the root of the tree, but it has not been summoned for duty. There is hope because the one who came was humble. He did not consider his equality with God as something to be exploited. Rather, he took the form of a servant and became obedient unto death.[3] He was humble, transforming the cross from a symbol of shame into the gateway of grace. And because of his humility in his ministry that led to his death, "God exalted him to the highest place and gave him name that is above every name and at that name every knee should bow in heaven and on earth and under the earth, and every tongue shall confess that he is Lord."[4]

That's the only name I place above every other name. "That's the name I love to hear, I love to sing its worth. It sounds like music in my ear, the sweetest name on earth."[5] Oh, how I love Jesus, because he first loved me. There is no danger in humbly following the one who loved us first. ✤

NOTES

1. Matthew 3:2, NIV.
2. Romans 12:3, NIV.
3. See Philippians 2:5-8.
4. Paraphrase of Philippians 2:9-11.
5. Paraphrase of "Oh How I Love Jesus." Words by Fredrick Whitfield, 1900.

THE DEIVISION OF MUSIC AND ARTS

FRIENDSHIP MISSIONARY BAPTIST CHURCH—CHARLOTTE, NC

DR. CLIFFORD A. JONES, SR., SENIOR PASTOR
MR. TONY MCNEILL, MINISTER OF MUSIC AND ARTS
MR. D. J. BOYD, ASSISTANT MINISTER OF MUSIC AND ARTS

2006 CHURCH MUSIC & WORSHIP SUMMIT

Wednesday, November 8 --- Sunday, November 12, 2006

IN THE SHAPE OF SCRIPTURE

DR. ROSEPHAYNE D. POWELL
Professor of Music
Auburn University (Auburn, AL)

DR. WILLIAM C. POWELL
Professor of Music
Auburn University (Auburn, AL)

DR. LEO H. DAVIS, JR.
Minister of Music
ississippi Blvd. Christian Church (Memphis, TN)

MIN. KEVIN B. JAMES
Director of Worship
St. Stephens Baptist Church (Louisville, KY)

DR. TONY LEACH
Professor of Music
Penn State University
(State College, PA)

*SPECIAL GUESTS
FRIENDS OF THE GROOM
Christian Theater Arts Ministry
(Terrace Park, OH)

. . . OTHER OUTSTANDING FACILITATORS TO BE ANNOUNCED!!!!!!!

2006 SUMMIT PREVIEW

· 2006 Required Reading/Textbook: *WORSHIP IN THE SHAPE OF SCRIPTURE* by F. Russell Mitman
· Varied Interest Sessions, Panel Discussions, Small Group Talks, Hands-on Instruction, and Piano Lab
· Pipe Organ Dedicatory Concert featuring FMBC Principal Organist R. Monty Bennett and Guests
· Congregational HymnSing led by Dr. Tony Leach, featuring traditional, contemporary, metered (lined) hymn singing at its best!
· Ministry and Worship Expo & On-Site Bookstore
· Exciting "New Music" Packet
· **NEW FOR 2006:** Classes / Sessions for Children & Youth and Advisors (Saturday)
· ONLINE REGISTRATION AVAILABLE *JUNE 1st.* REGISTER EARLY AND SAVE!!!!!

REGISTRATION LIMIT: 500 PARTICIPANTS! First Come, First Served!

VISIT www.churchmusicsummit.net FOR FULL DETAILS, ON-LINE REGISTRATION,
AND TO BE ADDED TO THE MAILING LIST.

Telephone: 704-392-0392, ext. #117 Fax: 704-927-1131 Email us at: info@churchmusicsummit.net

MAKE PLANS TO ATTEND! DO NOT MISS IT!

w w w . c h u r c h m u s i c s u m m i t . n e t

A MESSAGE from the Original Promise Keepers

BENITA LEWIS

Exodus 1:15-17, NRSV

The king of Egypt said to the Hebrew mid-wives, one of whom was named Shiphrah and the other Puah, "When you act as mid-wives to the Hebrew women, and see them on the birthstool, if it is a boy, kill him; but if it is a girl, she shall live." But the midwives feared God; they did not do as the king of Egypt commanded them, but they let the boys live.

I've always found the Book of Exodus to be a book of intrigue. However, this winter as I began to study the book deeper, I was properly introduced to the midwives Shiphrah and Puah, a Hebrew mother, her daughter, and an Egyptian princess. Obviously, these women have always been present in the Exodus story, but this time their presence was radically different. You see, in this recent encounter, their story was transformed from a theological perusal to a very personal discovery because I was able to connect the five women's context to my personal struggle. These five women who sheltered, saved, and nurtured Moses were now more meaningful than ever before, because they reminded me of me and the host of black mothers, grand-mothers, teachers, childcare providers, church sisters, and mentors who nurture, protect, and keep black boys. I now see that I am a small link in a chain of women who are single-handedly ordained to nurture, pro-tect, and keep the very lives of black boys.

Corporately we (as black women) stand with the midwives, the Hebrew mother and daughter, and the Egyptian princess to protect God's promise. We, like our ancient counterparts, are the PROMISE KEEPERS! It is my belief that because our lives and stories are so similar, it is as if they are speaking to us and us to them. Let

Benita Lewis is a third-year student at Wesley Theological Seminary in Washington, D.C. She is an itinerant deacon in the African Methodist Episcopal Church.

me share with you a letter I wrote to them and what they said in response.

DEAR ORIGINAL PROMISE KEEPERS:

I must begin this letter by making a formal apology. I have read the accounts of your extraordinary works many times, yet I've not paid much attention to you or your stories. I've spent much of my time focusing on Moses, the burning bush, the plagues produced by Yahweh, and the deliverance of your people through the Sea. And yet I've overlooked the enormous impact that you had on the deliverance of Israel. Please forgive me—for not acknowledging you and the brave intelligence you used to keep Israel's promise and deliverance alive through the baby Moses. Thank you for looking beyond yourselves, your differences, your situations, and your fears! I appreciate and celebrate each of you!

This time when I read your story I was able to envision a strong connection between the five of you and the host of black women who nurture black boys in the twenty-first century. And today we summon the power of your strength, creativity, and intellect to complete the work that we've been called to do.

As I read through the following passages, Exodus 1:12-22 and 2:1-10, I notice that there were no males helping to keep Moses alive. Where was Moses' father? Didn't you resent having to carry out this difficult and dangerous work with no apparent help from the men?

Today, black women seem to stand in similar places. Our country's most recent census report reveals that single females rear more than 50 percent of black children in America. Therefore single mothers, grandmothers, female teachers and caregivers, mentors, and church sisters influence the majority of black boys. Oftentimes we are expected to com-

plete a tremendous task with very little male support. How did you do it?

We also stand at the very crossroads where you seemed to stand when you were faced with the odious task of keeping Moses alive. You had to stand against the insurmountable forces of Pharaoh, and so do we. Exodus 1:16-22 describes the very blatant attack that Pharaoh mounted against Hebrew boys. Just as Pharaoh sought to snuff out the lives of the Hebrew boys, a similar attack is being made on the lives of black boys in America.

We struggle with new pharaohs. Our pharaohs don't sit on thrones in great palaces, but they do have leather chairs in a white mansion. And there are other major powers, principalities, and rulers of darkness. These powers are intricately hidden in vast systems designed to eradicate black boys.

One attack by our pharaoh is the current education system that fails to meet the needs of black boys once they are over the age of eight. Boys become frustrated with the way they are educated and begin to drop out of school at alarming rates. Once black boys drop out of school, Pharaoh raises his ugly head through drugs and other illicit offerings. Another trick of the enemy is gang affiliation and violence. The final blow to black boys by Pharaoh is our complex and privatized prison system. While blacks are a small percentage of the overall population of the United States, an overwhelming number of the men are in the penal system are black.

Pharaoh seems to be devastating the black community's entire way of life through drugs, gangs, and high incarceration rates among black males. However, you were under similar pressures and so I have to ask you, how do we as black women support black boys when the odds seem so insurmountable? How do we nurture them into the men that God has destined them to be? My sisters, I believe that

God will use the experience of your words to empower us as we face the challenges of the twenty-first century. We need to hear a word from the Lord through you.

Urgent,

A Modern-day Promise Keeper

And in reply, they blessed me when they wrote back the following:

DEAR MODERN-DAY PROMISE KEEPERS:

Thank you for taking the time to write to us. We appreciate the fact that you have noticed and acknowledged our struggle and contribution to the deliverance of Israel. However, we must admit that it didn't seem so grand a gesture at the time. I guess we assumed that we were doing what had to be done—we've heard through the cosmos that your generation says it this way, "A sista got to do what a sista got to do!"

We can't speak to your questions regarding the whereabouts of Moses' father. We were so busy attempting to accomplish the most important thing (keeping Moses alive) that we didn't have the energy to focus on his father. We encourage women in your generation to summon all of their energies to get children the resources they need. Do it now or pay for it later. It's essential that children eat healthy food, have adequate clothing, shelter, and medical care. It is imperative that the proper means be set aside to that end. But in the *meantime*, don't waste your energy, spirit, and time getting angry and feeling resentful about the whereabouts of men. You must use the resources at your disposal to save the lives of black boys.

You described the new pharaohs that reside in the twenty-first century—they appear to be a mighty force with which to reckon. However, we feel as though some of the strategies we used may be helpful to you in your mission to save black boys. We ask that you reflect on Exodus 2:10. Here you read that our sister, the princess of Egypt, was in Pharaoh's palace, and she helped to preserve the life of Moses. Sometimes the promise has to seek refuge in the enemy's palace. Don't be so quick to abandon those school systems—aren't there some people there and some who can go there to help nurture black boys? There must be some programs designed within the power structure that can speak to the needs of black boys. If not, why don't you create them? You will remember that Moses' mother designed a vessel herself that was the kickstart to Moses' salvation.

Black mothers must consistently support black boys as they navigate their way through your school systems. You see, your job is not done just in the beginning, but you have to nurture after you save. The Bible says that God gave Moses' Hebrew mother direct influence and access to the child before he went to live in the enemy's house (Exodus 2:7-9). You must nurture and equip black boys with everything you know to be right and claim access to them even while they reside in the palace of the enemies.

Yes, it feels as though the concerns facing black boys seem insurmountable. It seems too much for human hands to handle. While you protect, nurture, and keep black boys, know that God is the only power that can propel them into the awesome men required to transform your generation. It was not until Moses had a burning bush experience that he began to move into the arena God intended just for him.

Finally, as—what did you call us? oh yes!—the Original Promise Keepers, we feel your pain, struggles, and concerns. As you keep struggling, remember the promise and your purpose. You must focus your attention on the preservation of black boys—even when it appears that all help has gone. Hold on to the promise. If you read Exodus close-ly, you noticed that God doesn't speak until Exodus 3:4, and at that point he speaks to an adult Moses. We were doing the work of God in chapters 1 and 2 without hearing the voice of God. All we had was the promise made to Abraham, Isaac, and Jacob. Please tell your sisters that sometimes keeping the promise of God requires that you believe in the promises of God, without even hearing the voice of God.

Black women, keep the faith, and go in strength. Not in your own might, but that of God and the collective power of the sisterhood.

With sisterly concern,

The Original Promise Keepers

P. S. Please encourage the black boys for us by letting them know that it is our belief that God has made a new decree—that black boys shall live and not die. He has also given them a future and a hope. In their futures they shall rise up and speak truth to injustice. They shall go before Pharaoh on behalf of their people. They will posses the courage to fight Goliath. They will preside over great kingdoms. They will prophesy to dead situations, and they will live again. When life has counted black boys out and determined that they are null and void with no hope of survival, they shall obtain resurrection power, and they will rise in the power of God Almighty.

Now that I've finished reading their letter, the message to all Promise Keepers is clear. I share it in love with you today: "Our boys shall surely live and not die!" ✤

THE WORLD Is a Ghetto

SYLVIA MOSELEY

THE AFRICAN AMERICAN**PULPIT** FALL 2006

Luke 17:14-16, NRSV

When he saw them, he said to them, "Go and show yourselves to the priests." And as they went, they were made clean. Then one of them, when he saw that he was healed, turned back, praising God with a loud voice. He prostrated himself at Jesus' feet and thanked him. And he was a Samaritan.

During the 1960s and '70s, songs with lyrics that talked about the ghetto were popular. When Lou Rawls sang a song called

Sylvia Moseley graduated in May 2006 with her Master of Divinity from Payne Theological Seminary in Wilberforce, Ohio.

"Tobacco Road" that portrayed abuse, neglect, and poverty, we all knew he was singing about the ghetto. The group War won awards with a song called "The World Is a Ghetto." And now twenty-first century hip-hop culture spends much of its time, rhythm, and rhyme glorifying life in the ghetto.

What comes to mind when you hear the word *ghetto*? Do we see only black or brown faces, or do we think in colors that run the gamut of the human race: white, yellow, red, and everything in between? I mean, what color is ghetto? We say things like "that's so ghetto" and "this is so ghetto," our voices dripping with derision and contempt, implying that being from the ghetto is not a good thing, while in reality many of us are only one generation removed from the ghetto. But the truth of the matter is that some of us feed our own need to feel superior by looking down on people in the ghetto.

You see, America's new pastime is entertaining itself watching the pained and broken people from the ghettos of urban and rural America—watching them crash and burn on "reality" TV. For a plane ticket and hotel room, people expose the gaping wounds of their lives to Maury or Jerry while the networks and talk-show hosts make millions. This is a new twist on exploitation of the poor. No, this is not a simply a new and modern-day phenomenon; historically even the church has participated in separating and humiliating groups they tagged as outsiders. Sixteenth-century Venice established the first ghetto. It was an area set apart for Jews and established to placate the Roman Catholic Church who had already forced the expulsion of Jews from much of Western Europe. During the next three centuries, ghettos for Jews were established in most of the countries of Western Europe. These ghettos were surrounded by walls, and the gates were locked at night. In many instances Jews were compelled to wear identifying insignia anytime they went outside the ghettos. Webster's dictionary defines *ghetto* as "a portion of a city in which members of a minority group live because of legal, social, or economic pressure."

My brothers and my sisters, allow me to suggest that this definition of a ghetto is somewhat limited. You see, the rich are a minority—20 percent of the population owns 80 percent of the wealth; they live in secluded portions of the city and put gates around their estates; they tend to associate only with each other; and they wear symbols of wealth as identifying insignia. If we allow ourselves to think outside the box and apply the definition at face value concerning where the ghetto is, who lives in the ghetto, and what a ghetto

looks like, then we'll see that Hollywood can be a ghetto, Beverly Hills can be a ghetto, and Park Avenue can be a ghetto. In fact, the pop group War said it right—the world *is* a ghetto!

In our Scripture, the men who lived on the outskirts of the Samaritan village were a minority group. They had ragged, rotted, filthy-smelling clothing that identified them as marginalized. They themselves are shouting "Unclean! Unclean!" to announce their coming and the need to avoid them. Their physical condition of leprosy landed them on the bottom rung of the socioeconomic ladder. They were in the ghetto. Their condition was chronic and incurable.

The Scripture tells us that Jesus passed through Samaria on his way to Jerusalem. This was not the first time in this Gospel that Jesus had gone to Samaria. Chapter 9, verses 51-56 recount that Jesus and the disciples were not received by the Samaritans. James and John wanted to wage a campaign similar to the "Shock and Awe" campaign America visited upon Iraq. But Jesus refused to allow them to punish the many for the sins of the few. Samaria was a place where Jews were hated, and Jews felt the same about the Samaritans. Jews would take the long way to Jerusalem rather than go through Samaria. But Jesus went a second time to a place that Jews went out of their way to avoid.

Jesus came to tear down generational walls of hatred that separate and to build bridges toward reason and reconciliation. Well, if Jesus wouldn't give up on healing the ghetto, then let me share with you three things we need to do if we are to take healing to the ghetto.

The first thing we need to do if we are to take healing to the ghetto is to make ourselves available. At the beginning of Luke 17, Jesus was teaching his disciples about faith and forgiveness. They asked Jesus to "increase our faith," so Jesus took them on a field trip to give them a lesson in faith. He made himself available to people who would never come to the temple. He made himself available to people who had already rejected him once. He made himself available to people whose condition of pain and suffering fused them into a community held together by shame. Just as Jesus made himself available to people whom society said didn't deserve any better than what they had, so we, as children of the King, must make ourselves available on the street corners. We must be available in the schools. We must be available in the jails. We must be available in the nursing homes. We must be available to hear the cry of hurting people.

That brings me to my next point. The second thing we must do is incline our ear of mercy to the cries of the hurting. We must hear like God hears if we are to take healing to the ghetto. When God heard the cry of Ishmael and Hagar in the wilderness, God provided living water, hope, and a future for them. When God heard the cry of Israel, God sent Moses to tell Pharaoh, "Let my people go." When God heard the cry of segregated Negroes, God sent Howard Thurman to say Jesus identified with the disinherited. God sent Rosa Parks to say no to injustice; God sent Malcolm to tell us it was either the ballot or the bullet, and Martin King to weave a dream for people who only knew what it was like when a dream was deferred. When my God hears the cry of God's people, the walls of Jericho come crashing down! We must pray for the ears of God to hear the cry of hurting people. We must pray for the mercy of Jesus. The men cried, "Jesus, have mercy on us!" Jesus intervened in the affairs of a broken, wounded, foreign community, and Jesus gave them what they asked for: mercy.

The potential problem with this intervention is when it is done to gain political or financial gain. For instance, since 1890 our

national policy has led us to intervene 135 times in the affairs of foreign communities. However, in most cases we did it not just to dispense mercy but to gain politically. When the people of Haiti cried for mercy, we gave them the dictatorship of Duvalier. When the people of Nicaragua cried for mercy, we gave them the brutality of the Somoza regime financed by money from crack cocaine. When the Iranians cried for mercy, we replaced a corrupt government with the ruthless Shah and family. When the business interests in Chile cried out to us, we toppled the government of Allende and replaced it with a sadistic murderer named Pinochet. And we supported the nightmare in Iraq called Saddam Hussein before Saddam became expendable. Yet when we attempt to critique the policies of our government, we hear, "America: love it or leave it."

Aren't you glad that God is unlike the government? Jesus did not allow the idolatrous nationalism of Israel or the seeking of political power and positioning of the leaders of his day keep him from taking the truth of God to show mercy to the ghetto. When Jesus' flesh said no, his divinity said yes, and Jesus showed mercy to a Canannite woman whose daughter was possessed. The mercy of Jesus told the lepers they had to put on faith and ignore their condition to get to their deliverance.

This brings me to my final point. If we are to take healing to the ghetto, then we must live like we believe the Word of God. We must not be afraid to show ourselves, to say to the world, "Look, Satan thought he had me, but Jesus lifted me. I almost lost my mind, but Jesus held me. I wanted to take my own life, but Jesus kept me." We must be willing to go to the ghetto and show our scars—the same way Jesus came back to the disciples and showed them his scars. Jesus will take our testimony and use it to help someone stand in the face of adversity.

The one Samaritan came back, fell down at Jesus' feet, worshiped, and thanked God. The Samaritan was the outsider, the non-Jew, and the outsider was the only one who got it. He understood that he was healed not because he deserved it but because of God's grace and mercy. The unmerited favor of God caused the Samaritan to break out in praise and gratitude.

When you have been dragged through the mud of life, when you have been through hell and brought out, you are eager to give God praise and thanks. When you have been forgiven much, you want to give your whole self to the Lord.

Jesus is using this lesson in faith to teach his church to go after the outsider. Jesus is telling us to go after the dope dealer who has a pocket full of death, the government officials who turn a blind eye to drugs coming into the country, the murderer on death row, the technicians who will put the needle in the arm of the murderer on death row, the CEOs who know cigarettes cause cancer and market them anyway, the politicians who lied about weapons of mass destruction. Jesus is saying, "I came to the ghetto for all of you." There is room at the cross for you. Give God glory, and tell someone what the Lord has done for you he can do for them. ✢

A Glimpse of GLORY

DEXTER U. NUTALL

THE AFRICAN AMERICAN**PULPIT** FALL 2006

Luke 9:28-31, NIV

About eight days after Jesus said this, he took Peter, John and James with him and went up onto a mountain to pray. As he was praying, the appearance of his face changed, and his clothes became as bright as a flash of lightning. Two men, Moses and Elijah, appeared in glorious splendor, talking with Jesus. They spoke about his departure, which he was about to bring to fulfillment at Jerusalem.

One of the most fascinating things to me about God is the specific purpose with which God orchestrates things. God has a predefined, preordained intention for every-

Dexter U. Nutall is a student at the Samuel DeWitt Proctor School of Theology at Virginia Union University. He is an ordained member of the ministerial staff at New Bethel Baptist Church in Washington, D.C.

thing, including each of our lives. Perhaps Jeremiah 1:5 says it best when God said, "Before I formed you in your mother's womb, I knew you." Yes, all of us have a particular design, a specific purpose, and a destiny that God intended when he formed us.

Yet somehow God requires a level of energy and effort from us in order for us to maximize our God-ordained potential. What an interesting concept potential is. It is essentially a glorified *maybe*. Potential is the unfulfilled promise that lies within you. It is what God intended for you. It is the unseen that sets the stage for what could take place in you.

Let me explain it this way. If you are anything like me, when you get in the driver's seat of a car you have never driven, one of the first things you do is observe the speedometer. You do this because in doing so you are able to discover exactly how fast the car is capable of going. But just because the speedometer says that the car *can* go 100 mph does not mean the car will ever reach 100 mph. It means that the manufacturer designed the car so that it is capable of reaching 100 mph. It means that 100 mph is the car's potential. Whether the car actually reaches 100 mph will be determined by who is driving the car. If some of us are driving, that car will come a lot closer to its potential than if others of us are driving. But the potential of the car is the same no matter who is driving.

And this is where a problem arises, because if we are honest with ourselves, there are moments when seeds of skepticism and suspicion creep into our consciousness about God's design for our lives. Because as learned as you are, as anointed as you are, as sanctified as you are, as theologically astute as you are, if you're honest, the thought crosses your mind every now and then whether you are capable of doing what you say you've been called to do. Or maybe I'm the only one who questions whether I'm the one that God called to preach, whether I'm the one God called to teach, whether I'm the one God called to serve, whether God can even save somebody like me—with all the things I've done to offend him. And when you find yourself in this dilemma, something has to happen to convince you that your potential is worth reaching. Because in any sort of progress, there will inevitably be a measure of struggle. The interesting thing is that whatever convinces you that your potential is worth pursuing is inevitably the same something that sustains you while you are struggling to reach it.

That is the exactly the place where we find Peter, James, and John in this text: looking for something to sustain them while they pursued the fulfillment of their potential and God's destiny for their lives. It was these three—Peter, James, and John—who formed the inner circle of the disciples. It was Peter, James, and John who were involved in some of the defining moments of Jesus' ministry. They observed some of the greatest miracles firsthand. They were with Jesus when he went to the garden of Gethsemane. They were as close to Jesus as anyone. They were his boys, his aces, his dawgs. The curious thing about this episode is that there must have been people in and about town who had no idea who Jesus was, people who had not heard Jesus preach. Surely, there were still people in the land who had not seen Jesus heal by the touch of his hand, people who did not know that the savior had come. Yet Jesus took people with whom he was familiar to the top of the mountain. In fact, Jesus took the three disciples closest to him to observe his glory. The question is why did Jesus allow the inner circle—folks who presumably knew who Jesus was and what Jesus could do—to experience his glory?

The first reason Jesus allowed Peter, James, and John to experience his glory was to show them he was more than even they understood him to be. Peter, James, and John were of Jewish descent. The Jews were expecting a conquering king to be their savior. As a matter of fact, the Bible tells us that after observing the miracles, the Jews tried to make Jesus king. And Jesus' refusal of all the accolades was perplexing to them. The fact that Jesus didn't call down fire on the Samaritans when they rejected him was confusing. They were so entrenched in tradition that they could not imagine that the God of Israel would send a suffering servant to be their savior.

Isn't that just like us—trying to make God conform to what we think God ought to be and do. God is busy trying to bless you, and you are busy putting God in a box so you can be blessed when you want, how you want, and with what you want. But it's when we open ourselves to experience the fullness of God that he shows us his glory. It's when we are in a pinch that God is able to expose himself to us in a way he has never done before. It's not a matter of whether God is capable. The question is whether we are prepared to see his glory.

Many of us are like Moses when he met God at the burning bush. We have not experienced enough of God's capacity to know how to describe God. So when Moses asked God who should he tell Pharoah sent him, God said just tell him you were sent by "I am." I like that because it's a description of the very essence of God. It means that God is entirely self-existent. Totally self-sufficient. It means that God is whatever you need God to be. Do you need God to be love? God says, "I am." Do you need peace? God says, "I am." Do you need provision? God says, "I am." You can fill in the blank for yourself. Whatever you need, God says, "I am."

That's the problem that the intelligentsia has with God. The intelligentsia has a problem with anything that can't be fully understood. But God's existence transcends our understanding. God does not exist in time; God orchestrates time. God is not a matter subject to proof or evidence; God is the standard by which truth is determined. That's why it doesn't matter how long you've been in church. There are some things about God that you just don't know yet. Paul says, "Now unto him who is able to do exceeding abundantly above all you can ask or even think."[1] That means God is more than just a car. God is more than just a house. God is more than just a rent payment. God is more than the clothes on your back and the food on your table. God is more than a bridge over troubled waters. When we really begin to understand God, we'll let God out of the box

and let God be all God is. Jesus allowed Peter, James, and John to experience his glory to show them he was more than they understood him to be.

But it was not only that! Jesus allowed the inner circle to experience his glory because he needed them to understand that there would be times when his countenance would *not* shine. These three had been with Jesus during some of the lowest points of his life. They had observed the unpleasant exchanges between Jesus and the Pharisees. They had sensed Jesus' sorrow when he was rejected by those who said they loved him. They sensed the pain in Jesus when he declared that birds have nests and foxes have holes, but the Son of Man has nowhere to lay his head. And it was in the midst of this miserable maze of experiences that Jesus took them on a mountain to pray. There, he showed them his glory. I would imagine that part of the awe that these three experienced up on that mountain resulted from the fact that, while they saw a glorified Jesus up on the mountain, most of the time they had been with Jesus, his face had not been shining. While they were working in the field, while they were ministering in the streets, while they were doing the grunt work, Jesus' countenance was not shining.

We need to learn that while we are on the road toward reaching the potential that God has placed in each of us, there will be times when it seems as if God's countenance isn't shining. There will be times when it feels like God has left us alone. When it seems like God has abandoned us. When we think God has kicked us to the curb. You know that you're maturing in your relationship with God when you can't feel God, but you know he's there.

It's like when you play peek-a-boo with a child. When you play peek-a-boo with an infant, you can cover your face with a napkin, and that infant will believe that you've disappeared. But as children grow older, they come to realize that even though they can't see your face, they can take their little fingers and move the napkin to find you were there all the time. When you really get to know God, you embrace the fact that even when the circumstances suggest otherwise, even when darkness seems to mask his presence, when your senses tell you there's nowhere to go and there's nowhere to turn— when you don't have a friend and you can't find anyone to turn to—that's the moment that God's right by your side. Because God's presence isn't based on your feelings; it's based on your faith.

That's why you can have peace in the midst of your chaotic condition. That's what sustains you while you're trying to reach your potential. Even at midnight, you can sing with Paul and Silas that "He walks with me and he talks with me and tells me I am his own."[2] You can rejoice even when it appears that God's face isn't shining. Jesus allowed the inner circle to experience his glory so they would know there would be times that they would not see the shining countenance of God.

But finally, notice something. The text says that not only did the inner circle see a transformed Jesus, but they also saw a transformed Moses and a transformed Elijah. That's significant. You see, Peter, James, and John understood that Jesus was different. But they could identify with Moses and Elijah. Moses and Elijah were regular men, just like they were. Moses and Elijah had issues just like they had. They had heard about Moses and his stuttering problem. They had heard that Moses was a murderer but was still used by God. They had heard about the fearful Elijah who ran to find a hiding place even after God had given him

victory. And yet there they were, up on the mountain with Jesus, appearing in glory. That's when Peter, James, and John understood that what you are now is only a glimpse of what you shall become.

I live in Washington, D.C., but I attend seminary in Richmond, Virginia. What that means is that every weekend I have to drive down I-95 South to Richmond and back, sometimes in the same day. Four hours of driving in a cramped car. Four hours of lonely highway with no one to talk to but God. It's a grueling drive. It's a lonely drive. And there are days when I just don't feel like making the trip. Sometimes as I'm driving, I can feel the weariness in my body and the fatigue tempting me to pull over. But what helps me is that they have these signs on the side of the road that tell me exactly how much farther I have to reach my destination. Every time I see a sign, it tells me I'm closer than I was before. I may not be there yet, but I'm headed in the right direction and I'm closer than I used to be! Somebody needs to go ahead and run right now!

I know it's tough. I know you're struggling to fulfill your purpose. I know there are doubters who question your call. I know it seems that God has ignored your prayers. But every now and then God will give you a sign, a glimpse of glory to let you know that you're headed in the right direction and you're closer than you used to be. Is there anybody here that can say, "I might not be all that I want to be and I might not be all that I could, but God has shown me a sign and I thank God that I ain't what I used to be"? Touch somebody and say, "I've seen a glimpse of God's glory!" ❖

NOTES
1. See Ephesians 3:20.
2. "In the Garden." Words and Music by C. Austin Miles (1868–1946).

DON'T Settle!

KIMBERLY C. ROGERS

Exodus 14:12-16, KJV

Is not this the word that we did tell thee in Egypt, saying, Let us alone, that we may serve the Egyptians? For it had been better for us to serve the Egyptians, than that we should die in the wilderness. And Moses said unto the people, Fear ye not, stand still, and see the salvation of the LORD, which he will shew to you to day: for the Egyptians whom ye have seen to day, ye shall see them again no more for ever. The LORD shall fight for you, and ye shall hold your peace. And the

LORD said unto Moses, Wherefore criest thou unto me? speak unto the children of Israel, that they go forward: But lift thou up thy rod, and stretch out thine hand over the sea, and divide it: and the children of Israel shall go on dry ground through the midst of the sea. (Exodus 14:12-16)

As we consider the plight of the Israelites in today's text, I'd like us to ponder a few pertinent questions in light of our circumstances today: What has quenched our righteous indignation, dimmed our fire, halted our progression, and stopped our forward motion? What has made us become content with remaining where we are? Why has the status quo become acceptable? Why are we satisfied with business as usual? For if we know we are God's chosen people, that he's made us in his image, and that he desires for us to be free

Kimberly C. Rogers received her Master of Theology degree from Princeton Theological Seminary in Princeton, New Jersey. She also serves in ministry at the Baptist Worship Center in Philadelphia, Pennsylvania.

We were not created to settle or be content with an existence that is based on anything less than God's design for us—to be free.

to worship him, then that ought to teach us that we were not created to settle or be content with an existence that is based on anything less than God's design for us—to be free. In fact, if we somehow find ourselves functioning in a status that is less than what God created us for, we should become restless, anxious, uneasy, uncomfortable, and just downright upset.

It saddens my heart to know that many of us have become satisfied in and with our oppression. We have become so content that if by chance we start progressing or moving forward, when something rises up in opposition—and it always will—we quickly decide that our lives would be better off if we just settle. We give up. We stop chasing our dreams because it's easier to pretend we don't want them than to deal with the risk, hardship, and possibility of failures that are inevitable in the pursuit of anything worth having.

We say: "It's okay to stay in an abusive relationship; at least I've got a roof over my head. It's okay to remain at that dead-end job; at least I get a paycheck every week. It's okay never to 'become' the church; at least I attend church. It's okay just to preach prosperity and personal piety; at least I've got some members. It's okay to shut up and say nothing while thousands are losing their lives in Iraq and Iran; at least I live in America where there is more opportunity."

I'm afraid that we have bought into our oppressors' visions and ingested their propaganda. We celebrate our oppressed state and think our oppression is not that bad because at least we've got some stuff. We now stand in contradiction to the old Negro spiritual, "Before I'd be a slave, I'd be buried in my grave, and go home to my Father and be free." And our lives now speak the same words of the Israelites: "Let us alone, that we may serve the Egyptians." In other words, let us settle.

We have become too cozy in and with our oppression. Although we may not want to hear it, we have to take some responsibility for our condition. For we've started to dress like our oppressors. We've started to like the food of our oppressors. We've started desiring their houses and their cars. And if that is not bad enough, some us have had the audacity to hold our noses in the air and boast about what we've got, because we think we are the best of the oppressed.

God has historically stood on the side of the marginalized, downtrodden, and oppressed. God is a God of not only individual but also corporate deliverance. Thus, I don't believe God just wants *me* to get a six-figure salary, so that *I* can get a nice car and drive *myself* out of the ghetto, but rather we should all work to rid ourselves of the social, economical, and political conditions that bring about a necessity for a ghetto. Rev. Martin Luther King Jr. said, "We are caught in an inescapable network of mutuality, tied in a single garment of destiny. Whatever affects one directly, affects all indirectly. Injustice anywhere is a threat to justice everywhere."[1]

Therefore, I can't believe it is God's will that we thrive to the point of complacency

Our real values are often revealed through our hardships.

in our oppression. I can't believe it is God's will for us to become satisfied with just living as the highest of the lowest, the richest of the poorest, nor the best of the oppressed of society! But, we have to take some responsibility for not always reaching back as we climb.

However, after first examining our own actions, we must also look at how the actions of others have contributed to our state of complacency. This is what happened to the children of Israel in our text. They marched out of Egypt in great joy and celebration. After more than 400 years of slavery, they had been set free. Freed to live in cities they did not build, drink from wells they did not dig, and eat from vineyards they did not plant. They were finally moving toward their destiny. But just when their dreams seemed attainable and the impossible seemed possible, they found themselves sandwiched between a dilemma and a difficulty. They looked ahead and saw the Red Sea. They looked behind and saw Pharaoh and his army. Somebody knows what I'm talking about. Every time you try to move forward you face a dilemma and difficulties sneak up from behind.

The children of Israel were in a dark hour. They began to second-guess their decision to leave their oppression. They may have left the physical place of their oppression, but the mentality of oppression had not left them; old thought patterns reemerged. Our real values are often revealed through our hardships. These Israelites had been taught since infancy that they were slaves, they were less than, and they should just settle. Pharaoh didn't just use constant govern-

ment surveillance, secret wire taps, secret police, or secret torture in secret prisons to intimidate the people—although our current presidential dictatorship has proven that this too is an effective method of control. Pharaoh knew that the best way to control the children of God was to brainwash them subtly into accepting their state of oppression.

Everything in that society socialized them to think and act like slaves. This started first by devaluing their personhood. There were subtle suggestions, which slowly eroded the humanity and personhood of the Israelites. The continual reinforcement of their devalued status reminded them that they were just ignorant slaves; they were just objects, they had no future, and they had no hope. They were socialized to accept their oppression the same way we are socialized to accept ours.

I am concerned that every time a video-girl "drops it like it's hot," some young girl is reminded that she's just an object. Every time a public school closes and after-school programs are cut because billons are given to causes the rich represent, our children are reminded they have no future. Every time the government puts on a smoke and mirror show and plays the point-the-finger-game while Katrina survivors still struggle with the devastating after-effects of the storm, we are all reminded that oppressed people are not considered good enough for our government to help.

The children of Israel internalized the oppressor's messages until those messages were transformed into subconscious values. Their personhood was placed in the hands of

Just because we may have settled, God has not!

those who would exploit it. Their humanity was stripped from them. They had been so dehumanized that the only way to try to regain their humanity was to adopt the norms of their oppressor. Norms that included hostilities hurled upon the folk who looked just like them! They internalized their oppressor's hatred for them and started hating themselves and their own kin. So, of course folk were acting like crabs in a barrel. We still see increasing rates of black on black crime. Folk that look like us, from our neighborhoods, sell us out for a handshake and photo-op with the president.

Devaluing someone's personhood makes it easier to get that person to settle. Devalued people have been taught to hate themselves and to value their oppressor more than their own people. When you devalue a group's personhood, you are diminishing their esteem and self-worth. You have manipulated them into believing they are not worth the cost it would take to move forward. Therefore, they settled because their personhood had been devalued.

Then, I believe the Israelites settled because their *history* was devalued. Not only was there a pharaoh who knew not Joseph during this time period, but there was also a people who knew not their own history. Denying any people firm groundings in their history is a calculated maneuver to produce folks who are easily led and manipulated by others. Hebrew history did not begin with their enslavement, but many Hebrews did not know this. If you leave it up to your oppressors to teach you your history, you will either be written out of it, or if included, only included as uncivilized

heathens in need of the oppressor's spiritual, intellectual, and moral prowess.

Knowing the true worth of our history is important for a number of reasons. Our history provides us with a track record that reminds us when we do run into dilemmas and difficulties that this is not the first time we've been here. If the children of Israel had known their history, they would have seen this wasn't the first hardship they had had to face. If they had known their history, they would have realized that this wasn't the first time they had had to pick up and leave a land by faith. If America knew world history, we would be careful because all empires built on world domination fall. If America knew our own history, we would have learned our lesson from other wars we had no business engaging in. If America knew our history, we wouldn't be trying to take other people's countries, destroy other people's cultures, and celebrate committing genocide under the umbrella of a flag and a cross!

Our history provides us with wise counsel. Our history provides us with precedent for survival. Our history provides us with a blueprint for hope. Our history teaches us that "through many dangers toils and snares, we have already come. 'Twas grace that brought us safe thus far and grace will lead us home."[2]

Devaluing a people's history leaves the door wide open for people to become crippled by fear. If you can devalue a people's history, they will not know who they are. They will not know from whence they have come. They will continually settle for living as less-than because they don't know that they don't have to! In order to keep the Israelites oppressed, the Egyptians devalued Israelites' personhood; then, they devalued their history.

Last, the Egyptians devalued the Israelites' God. During this time in Egypt's history, Pharaoh was viewed as being equal to a god. What Pharaoh said was law. The Israelites lived in a land where Pharaoh received great value while their God was devalued. Pharaoh reigned supreme. Imagine a land where patriotism is exalted over the church. The flag is exalted over the cross. Money is exalted over morals. Greed is exalted over grace. "I" is exalted over "we." Picture a land where you are constantly being told your God has no power. Oh, but no matter how much others try to devalue God, he is still omnipotent. Others may have *some* power, but God still has *all* power.

So, Moses opened his stammering mouth and said, "Stand still and see the salvation of the LORD." Then, God called Moses into his office for a consultation. Moses went back and stood before a devalued people, with a devalued history, and a devalued God. See, although the people had settled, God would not! God had a leader in Moses who was willing to look past the people's faults and see God's divine plan. Moses knew that these were God's chosen people, that God had made them in his image, and that God desired for them to be free to worship him. Thus, Moses wouldn't let the people return to the status quo and business as usual. Moses lifted his rod, stretched out his hands, and divided the sea.

Suddenly, the waters opened up. Suddenly, that thing that had dimmed their fire, halted their progression, and stopped their forward motion was removed. Moses lifted his rod—a rod is a stick or branch of a vine—he stretched out

his hands, and the sea divided. The Hebrew term used here for "divide" also gives us the meaning "to breakthrough." In other words, when the rod, the branch of the vine, was lifted and his hands were stretched out, there was a breakthrough!

That's not just good news for the children of Israel, but it is also good news for us today. Just because we may have settled, God has not! God had another leader who was willing to look past our faults and see God's divine plan. The Father instructed that leader— Jesus—thousands of years ago, to stretch out his hand and divide or give us a breakthrough. When he stretched out his hands on a cross at Calvary, he broke through the temple's veil and those once excluded were now included and all had instant access to the Father. When he stretched out his hands, he broke through and what was once just about religion became about relationship. He broke through time and divided it into B.C. and A.D. He broke through our sin and gave us salvation. He broke through our fear and gave us faith, took us from darkness to light, from sorrow to joy, and from death to eternal life. In Christ there is a breakthrough, so don't settle. Christ has cleared a path for us to go forth.

So, don't settle! Because of Christ, you can start that business. Don't settle! Because of Christ you can go back to school. Don't settle! Because of Christ you can leave that toxic relationship, apply for that program, write that grant, mentor a child, speak out about injustice, pick up the baton of civil rights, love your neighbors, lift up your brothers and your sisters, and preach the gospel. Don't settle! ✤

NOTES

1. Martin Luther King Jr., *Letter from a Birmingham Jail.* April 16, 1963.
2. "Amazing Grace," lyrics by John Newton, (1725–1807), paraphrased.

GOD SAYS SO...So Why Don't We?

HEIDI M. STEVENS

Isaiah 54:1, 6, NIV

"Sing, O barren woman, you who never bore a child; burst into song, shout for joy, you

who were never in labor; because more are

the children of the desolate woman than of her who has a husband," says the LORD...."The LORD will call you back as if you were a wife deserted and distressed in spirit—a wife who married young, only to be rejected," says your God.*

Week after week, millions of television viewers across the country wait in fanatic expectation for the latest installment of *American Idol*—who will Paula let slide, who will Simon slam, and who will Randy sacrifice? Just watching one audition episode lets you know that not all of the contestants can carry a tune, but you have to admit that they all have one thing in common: they all have nerve—an inner confidence that provides the belief that they should be there.

Somewhere down the line, at home, at school, or at church, a grandmother, a teacher, or a friend told them that they could sing—and they believed it. Someone told them that they could be whatever they wanted to be, and they received it. Someone told them that all they had to do was to see it, so they set out to achieve it. Even though many of them won't be the next *American Idol*, you can clearly see that there is something deep inside each of them that drives them to take hold of their dreams. They are tuned into a voice that whispers deep in their spirit, "Yes...you can do it!"

As I read and meditated on Isaiah 54:1-2, I had to wonder the same thing about the woman of Zion. Why would a woman who had a fruitless womb want to sing? Why would a stigmatized woman who had no hope of leaving a lasting legacy want to

Heidi M. Stevens is pursuing a Master of Arts in Theology at The Ecumenical Institute of Theology at St. Mary's Seminary in Baltimore, Maryland. She serves in ministry at Mt. Calvary African Methodist Church in Towson, Maryland.

**Why would a desolate woman even dare contemplate a glimmer
of expectation for a better life? After searching and searching
I realized that she did it because God said so.**

shout? Why would an isolated and maligned woman who was living in a hopeless, lifeless, and stressful situation want to raise her voice in joy? Why would a desolate woman even dare contemplate a glimmer of expectation for a better life? After searching and searching I realized that she did it because God said so.

Because God said so, she expected more! Because God said it, she had no problem believing that she would birth a multitude of spiritual children and could stretch her tents wide to accept the overflow that God was preparing for her. Because she had the word of God, she had no problem with thinking big and living large on the promises of God.

This Scripture speaks to the promises, hope, and expectation that God has spiritually spoken into each of our lives. So the question is, if God is speaking promises, hope, and expectation, why aren't many of us moving to take possession of the promises that God has planned for us from the beginning of time? Why aren't we living the Jeremiah 29:11 life that promises unlimited hope and a superfantastic future? I believe that we are not making a joyful noise into the land of fulfilled dreams because we don't *see* the promise, we don't *believe* the promise, and sometimes we don't *want* the promise.

Sometimes when God says so, we don't *see* the promise because we are too distracted to see with our natural eyes what God is really doing in the spiritual. We are so busy looking for a physical sign of progress or change that we lose hope and abort the vision that God so lovingly gave us. When God tells us to stretch our tents wide or to increase our faith, in essence the Lord is telling us to prepare ourselves in the spirit for the poured-out blessing that he wants to give us. But instead of stretching our faith and strengthening our resolve to make sure we are spiritually mature and physically prepared to handle the promise, we complain about our present tent and go looking for a better tent to stretch wide—or we keep our eyes on someone else's stretched-out tent to the point that we can't see and hear what God is instructing us to do.

Just think, if King David of the Old Testament had let his natural eyes deceive him, he would have abandoned his destiny as king and forfeited his position in the lineage of Jesus Christ. Saul, the first king of Israel, was already wearing the crown as David was being anointed by the prophet Samuel to rule over the children of Israel. The spiritually blind would waste time worrying about how all of this would play out. But perhaps David understood that God was working quietly behind the scenes. No one could see it in the natural, but God was moving to make sure that he had the right person on the throne. Just because you don't see yourself as a king or queen doesn't mean that God doesn't see you that way. He said that you are a royal priesthood, that you are the head and not the tail. Just because you aren't walking in promised places today doesn't mean that you won't be running in them tomorrow. You have to be able to see the promised blessing before you experience it. See it because God says so!

However, even though God says so, sometimes we don't *believe* it. God told Zion that they would spread out to the right and to the

Many of us are so laden with low-self esteem and self-hatred that we can't believe we deserve the riches that God has stored up for us.

left, that their descendants would dispossess nations and settle in desolate cities. God was telling them that they had a right to take authority over what he was going to give them. Many of us are so laden with low self-esteem and self-hatred that we can't believe we deserve the riches that God has stored up for us. We don't believe that God loves us and sent his only son, Jesus, to die on the cross just for us. But don't fall for the lies that the deceiver has spoken to you. You have to believe and live in expectation that you will reap the harvest that God has promised you.

We must walk in faith believing that the promises in the Word of God are not just for the the Bible-toting, the gold-cross-wearing, the blessed, the beautiful, or the highly favored. The promises are also for the marginalized, the criticized, the underappreciated, the neglected, the disrespected, and those of us who have messed up. We have to believe in the Christ who lives in us and through whom all things are made possible. When we believe in the power of Jesus, we must believe that through him we can be more than conquerors.

As God tells the people of Zion to get ready to be blessed, God also tells them not to be afraid or feel disgraced—that their mistakes and transgressions will be forgiven and they will be redeemed and loved. Now that's something to shout about! Because many times that is the one thing that keeps people from being all they can be in Christ. Sometimes we record our wrongdoings and keep them on instant replay. We keep rehearsing our history to the point that we can't receive the promises of today.

Then there are times when, even though God says so, we don't *want* to be what God has called us to be in the Kingdom. The prophet Jeremiah claimed that he was too young to warn Israel, and I thought that I was too timid to be God's messenger. But the shout is that God has a way of working things out. God will not only prepare you for your destiny, but he will also be with you when you move outside your comfort zone to take hold of the promise. So, step out in faith because God has provided the perfect example for us to follow. God has given us a Man who has taught us how to live outside our comfort zone to achieve the dream.

That man is Jesus, who at the age of twelve stepped out into the deep to declare the words of his Heavenly Father in the temple. It was Jesus who at thirty years old took on Satan in the wilderness to stand strong and to be all that he was meant to be, and it was Jesus who at the age of thirty-three stretched his arms wide on the cross and didn't hold back so that we could rise again from the ashes of shame, the devastation of rape, the trap of homosexuality, and the murderous consequences of crack-house living. From divorce and from bankruptcy you can rise; from abuse and discrimination you can rise; from disappointment, depression, and yes, even from degradation, you can and will rise!

Because of Jesus, we can see the promise when the situation looks cloudy; we can believe the promise when everyone else doubts; and we can walk in the promise because we can do all things through Christ who strengthens us. We can do all this and more, because God says so! ✢

Considerations on THE CROSS

JASON LAWRENCE TURNER

1 Corinthians 1:18, NRSV

For the message about the cross is foolishness to those who are perishing, but to us who are being saved it is the power of God.

The church of Corinth is at the crossroads of culture. Consequently it is confronted concurrently with conflict and controversy concerning Christ, Calvary, and the cross. Many misunderstandings, misrepresentations, and misinterpretations are muddying this message of our martyred Master and Messiah. This presents a paradox.

Jason Lawrence Turner is a senior at Yale Divinity School in New Haven, Connecticut.

And it was here at this collision of cultures that Paul was grappling with the paradox of the cross. Paul recognized that there was a Grecian and Jewish presence in the community struggling to glean the grace and glory which had been invested in the cross. The cross, for them, was foolishness. It was merely two pieces of wood intersecting at a perpendicular point so as to form four 90-degree angles. It was an execution for hardened criminals, a perfected method of capital punishment, the ancient equivalent to the modern-day electric chair. It represented a shameful and humiliating death. But through the redemptive redefinition by Jesus Christ, Paul was able to share that the meaning of the cross does not rest with those who are perishing, but he encouraged us, writing, "but unto us which are saved it is the power of God."

But through the redemptive redefinition of Jesus Christ, Paul was able to share that the meaning of the cross does not rest with those who are perishing, but he encouraged us, writing, "but unto us which are saved it is the power of God."

For those of us who are the redeemed of the Lord, the cross is much more than wood assembled for the purpose of execution. It is salvation for the sinner, grace for the guilty, and hope for the helpless. There is significance found in the horizontal and vertical dimensions that point to our future in heaven, our freedom from hell, and our fellowship with humanity. I submit that when you and I consider the cross, it grants us purpose for our lives, pardon for our lapses, and a plan for life everlasting!

Sisters and brothers, we have been designed and destined to live not only *for* a purpose but *on* purpose. We are not here for any arbitrary reason, but each of us is here on this earth on assignment. I can hear the cognitive conversation in the congregation from those who are wondering, "How can there possibly be a purpose for my life?" There are those who have had disappointing lives thus far and who believe that there is no reason for living. I am well aware that there are those who have had traumatizing experiences in life. Maybe you are a young black man who never knew your father and all that you know of him is what everyone else tells you about him. They say that he wasn't much of a man, and because he didn't amount to much in life, you're told you won't amount to much either. Or possibly you were born to parents who were not married at the time of your conception or birth, and you've been told your entire life that your birth was a mistake, that your concep-

tion was an accident. Sisters and brothers, although we go through trying times in life, we need to know that we're not here by accident or coincidence, but we're all here by the divine providence of God.

The cross empowers us to live on purpose because it makes us aware of the investment God made in humanity through the sacrifice of Jesus. God would not have given so much for that for which he had no purpose, plans, or intentions. The sacrifice of Jesus is a priceless, preemptive, and proven sacrifice. It's a priceless sacrifice in that Jesus is the only begotten Son of the Father. Jesus is the very best God had to offer to atone for our sins. Dietrich Bonheoffer said, "...it is costly because it cost God the life of his son....God did not reckon his Son too dear a price to pay for our life, but delivered him up for us."[1] If God had no use for us, he would have let us die in our sins, but he sent the very best that he had in order to purchase our redemption.

Not only is it a priceless sacrifice; it's also a preemptive sacrifice, for Revelation 13:8 tells us Jesus was a "Lamb slain from the foundations of the world." Before there was a who, what, when, or a where...before the Garden of Eden was arrayed with its beauty or the sun, moon, and stars were flung into the sky, Jesus had already died for our sins.

Furthermore, the sacrifice for our sins is a proven sacrifice. It's proven in that as sure as there are sinners in the world, the blood offered in this sacrifice still saves. From the 'hood to the house on the hill, the blood is proven to still save. But in that provision has been made for sin, we also know that because of the cross we can receive pardon for our lapses. If we would tell the truth, all of us would confess that we have sinned—just as Romans 3:23 says, "All have sinned…." And if the truth is told, since we have accepted Christ as our personal Savior and Lord of our lives, we have continued to make mistakes. Even when we make the best effort and try to do the right thing, we find ourselves as Martin Luther says, *simul justus et pecattor,* "at the same time justified and sinner."

We know we are forgiven, but we have many failures. Thank God we can consider the cross, and when we consider the cross, we are convicted that our failures are not eternally fatal, for Romans 5:8 proclaims, "But God commended his love toward us, in that, while we were yet sinners, Christ died for us."

We must remember that salvation is a process that begins with justification, through which God makes us as if we had no sin at all, freeing us from the penalty of sin. I can remember my first year of college being irresponsible and a bad steward of my cell phone use. There was an occasion where I exceeded my allotted minutes for the month and incurred charges I was not able to handle with my own financial resources. To make matters worse, I remember receiving a call from my cell phone service provider threatening to disconnect my service if I did not make a payment. In my frantic frenzy and frustration, I called my daddy, and because of my relationship with him, he did a number of things to resolve my situation. First, he paid the bill for me to keep me from being disconnected. Then he went to the provider and reasoned with them not to penalize me for my

negligence, and they granted me a clean slate. But finally, Daddy called the cell phone company again and arranged it from that point forward that the bill no longer came to me but it went straight to him.

That's what God the Father did for us through Jesus Christ at the cross! The Father paid for our sins. But he did not stop there; he pulled up our report, and took the blood of Jesus and "whited out" all of the charges we had incurred. But thank God he did not stop there. Because he knew we are vulnerable and weak creatures and subject to sin, he arranged it so that our sins are no longer charged to our account; they go straight to him. God paid my debt, wiped my slate clean, and then forwarded all of the bills to himself! Isn't that what Jesus did for all of us? In fact the songwriter took pen to paper and declared, "Jesus paid it all. All to him I owe. Sin had left a crimson stain. He washed it white as snow."[2]

He paid it all. No, I am not perfect, but I remind myself to "forever lift mine eyes to Calvary to view the cross where Jesus died for me. How marvelous the grace that caught my falling soul. He looked beyond my fault and saw my need."[3] That is what the cross is all about! For it was, "At the cross, at the cross. Where I first saw the light and the burden of my heart rolled away. It was there by faith I received my sight, and now I'm happy all the day!"[4] ✣

NOTES
1. Dietrich Bonheoffer. *The Cost of Discipleship* (New York: Macmillan, 1966), 48.
2. Elvina Hall. "Jesus Paid It All," *African American Heritage Hymnal* (Chicago: GIA Publications, 2001), 357.
3. Dottie Rambo. "He Looked beyond My Fault," *African American Heritage Hymnal* (Chicago: GIA Publications, 2001), 249.
4. Ralph Hudson and Issac Watts. "At the Cross," *African American Heritage Hymnal* (Chicago: GIA Publications, 2001), 264.

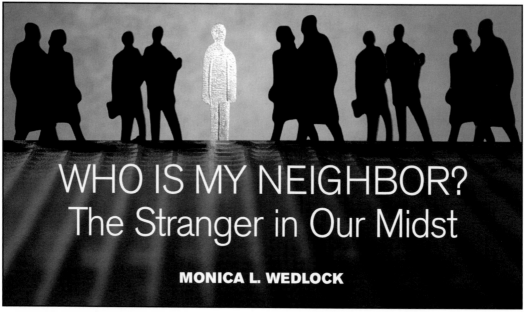

WHO IS MY NEIGHBOR?
The Stranger in Our Midst

MONICA L. WEDLOCK

Matthew 25:31-46, NIV

The king will reply, "I tell you the truth, whatever you did for the least of these brothers of mine, you did for me." (Matthew 25:40)

As we look around, we realize that the world is changing daily. Our children face new challenges; the family less and less resembles the traditional unit of husband, wife, and children; doors of opportunity are steadily opening for some, while others are losing their jobs. It seems like every day we face some natural or human disaster that shifts the hope we had for our future. Technology is advancing at the speed of light, and no longer do we know who lives next door.

Have you looked around lately at the world, and noticed all the things that are different? The people on your job change rapidly over a five-year time span; few people stay in the same job for twenty or thirty years these days. Look around at the mall sometime, and notice who is shopping and eating and going to the movies. And what about our neighborhoods? Every time the market shifts from a seller's to a buyer's market, we get new neighbors. Do you know who your neighbors are?

Hopefully, somewhere in the back of our minds we remember that community and family used to mean something to our grandparents and ancestors. *Community* and *family* were never terms that meant *my* house, *my* relatives and friends, *my* church, *my* job. Those terms also never meant *my* people, who look and act just like *me*. But somehow, our American psyche has created in us a pervasive and poisonous reality of individualism. History has told us that our struggle has been a struggle for all people, but somehow, we've started to live as if the harvest that you and I have reaped has simply been a harvest for *you and me*. We've even commemorated the Civil Rights Movement with liberation songs and services and quotes from speeches, believing that the

Monica L. Wedlock is a Master of Divinity student at Columbia Theological Seminary in Decatur, Georgia.

struggle was *just for us*, that the battle to liberate humanity is over, and we can now beat our swords into plowshares.

I challenge you to look around at the world today, sing those songs again, and listen more carefully to those speeches. Refrains like "Ain't Gon' Study War No More" sound a lot different when you watch the news and hear about the tragedy in the Middle East and the body count of innocent civilians and soldiers, reported and unreported. "We Shall Overcome" takes on new meaning when you consider the HIV/AIDS pandemic that plagues the world and continues to reach new proportions in the Motherland, Lady Africa. "Swing Low, Sweet Chariot" is heard with new ears when you hear the stories of refugees from Haiti, Cuba, and Latin America coming to the USA for freedom and new opportunities for their families. In case you don't remember, these are freedom songs—songs that gave us hope for a new day, but also songs that constantly remind us of our present reality.

We celebrate the life and legacy of Dr. Martin Luther King Jr., but honestly, we've forgotten what his life and legacy were really all about. Do we not know? Have we not heard that the liberation struggle of the Negro was not so we could have prestigious jobs, drive big fancy cars, and live in homes within gated communities? The liberation of the Negro was the fire-starter for the liberation of all people. There was never an instance when the civil rights leaders and activists stopped working after a single victory was won. I know we don't talk about it much, but King didn't just fight for blacks. He united with the union workers for fair wages for the poor and working class; he spoke out against the Vietnam War for the return of U.S. soldiers and peace for the

Vietnamese people; and he preached about his children not being judged by the color of their skin but by the content of their character. Why? So that all persons of *all* races, classes, and cultures would be treated with love and respect. Or has that part been left out of the story?

You may be wondering why I'm rehashing old stuff. What does this mean for us today? Well the truth is, I'm challenging us to take another look. We have a host of new struggles and fights for freedom in our midst; the battle *ain't* over. It never was over, but somehow we found false hope in what we've gained—or maybe we have gotten too tired to keep up the fight. But if you watch the news, read the paper, or listen to the voices around you—especially those who are being silenced—it will be more than evident that the hope is fading and we don't have time to be tired.

Look in the faces of hungry children; take note of those who have lost their jobs; reach out and touch the hand of someone next to you, and feel their struggle despite the smile on their face and their eloquent public prayers. The struggle for liberation *ain't* over.

In Luke 4, Jesus reads from the scroll of the prophet Isaiah saying, "The Spirit of the Lord is on me, because he has anointed me to preach good news to the poor. He has sent me to proclaim freedom for the prisoners and recovery of sight for the blind, to release the oppressed, to proclaim the year of the Lord's favor."

Present-day reality tells us that the sick are getting sicker, the poor are getting poorer, more people are dying, and the captive are not free. But why is this our present-day reality? Because we've given up and gotten complacent. We've begun to believe that those in need are lazy, uneducated, and lack

For Jesus, the other, the stranger, the marginalized, the destitute, the voiceless, the powerless, the nameless, and the faceless are all his neighbors.

vision. We've discounted their lives and their stories, and we've gone into our homes, locked our doors, and closed our blinds. We worship our little personal Jesus, and we pray for our personal blessings. We've become like the Israelites at the bottom of the mountain when Moses went up to see the Lord. We've gotten restless with the journey and started making our own golden calves and celebrating our own victories. Or maybe we are wandering in the wilderness because we've seen our enemies in the land and we believe their strength is just too great. We're up against systems and laws and ways of thinking that go back centuries upon centuries.

But if we keep believing the battle is over or there's too much standing in our way, what happens to our tomorrow? What's the fate of our children?

If you've been watching the news or reading the paper lately, you may have heard about the pending immigration legislation and the battle of the Latino community. The legislative talk is centered on our need for tougher Homeland Security policies and procedures, but the target singled out has been one community of people in particular. One bill proposes tougher enforcement of the already existing valid ID laws that prove citizenship or legal residency. On the surface, this doesn't pose a problem and actually isn't such an unfair request. But the next piece of legislation then redefines the parameters of those who benefit from basic social services, such as education and emergency healthcare. In other words, if someone is stopped for a traffic violation, police officers will ask for license, registration, and proof of residency or citizenship. If a five-year-old girl born in the U.S. goes to register for school and her last name is Sanchez, her parents will be asked to show proof of residency for her and for themselves. Based on their legal status, this young girl can be denied access to an education. Take a look around. What's the legal status of your neighbor?

You have ignored the stranger in our midst, and I have too. We have only been concerned with those around us when it benefits or affects us; otherwise, we go on with our lives without even seeing the people who are right in front of our faces. The Latino population has been singled out as the source of all of our problems, and we have sat back in agreement. But don't you remember when you, me, we were singled out? Even now, African Americans are blamed as the source of all the drug problems, murders, poverty, homelessness, unemployment, teenage births, and the list goes on. Today, the Latino community is being exploited through the use of their labor. We, too, were exploited for the very same reason.

Our collective history as people of color has been one of suffering, injustice, and divine hope. It has been our faith in Jesus as liberator that has brought us through today, and that reminds us to take another look at the story of Esther who was raised up and liberated "for such a time as this." Her uncle Mordecai had a perspective on the Hebrew reality that did not allow him to be comfortable with having raised Esther to be queen. He reminded her that her liberation was not for herself—but that she had been positioned to liberate God's people. Are we not hearers of the same prophetic voice? Have we not come this far and gained this position to help liberate others?

The text in Matthew 25, known as the parable of the sheep and the goats, points us to another way of understanding our role and responsibility to one another—and in particular, those who are our neighbors. We often think of our neighbors as those who physically live next door to us or those we go to school with—those we see on a regular basis. But I suggest to you that our neighbors are all those we come in contact with, in word or deed—and beyond. Yes, our neighbors can have names and faces that are familiar, but in light of the radical nature of the kingdom of God, more often our neighbors are those who remain nameless and faceless in our midst.

An initial reading of the focal text concludes that Jesus was talking about a day of final judgment when we will stand before the Lord and our lives will be recounted before us. This is a wonderful thought for some, but for many of us it can be quite terrifying when we think back on some of the things we have done—or haven't done for that matter. But today, I offer another reading of the text in light of our charge given by Jesus in Luke 4.

A second reading of the parable of the sheep and goats plays on the idea of the final judgment day, but with eyes into the future, we can correct our present. This parable is a prophetic word to us today about God's call for our lives. It tells us very specifically how we should live in the world with our neighbors. Verses 31-33 set up the scene in the heavenly court system in which God is the judge and we are on trial. What's unusual for us is that we don't get a chance to plead our

case and make our arguments before God this time; our actions during our life and how we lived out the gospel will speak on our behalf. Those on trial will be the rich and the poor, the liberated and the captive, the hungry and the well-fed, the dead and the living, the friend and the foe, the neighbor and those called the stranger.

The text tells us that the king will separate those before him—some to the left and others to the right. We are told that those on his right will be called blessed and invited to receive their inheritance. The king is very specific in his exposition as *he* pleads the case of those on the right. He makes no mention of battles they have fought or victories they have won. He doesn't mention the wealth they have accumulated or the high places of status they have attained. He doesn't even allude to the charities they have chaired or the money they have donated. He only points out the fact that these people to his right have offered their food and drink, welcomed the stranger in their midst, clothed the naked that passed by, nursed the infirm, and spent time with the captive. The irony in this trial is that those on the right become their own prosecutors. They cross-examine the judge by asking for proof of such deeds on their behalf. And the king speaks in their defense saying that there was no one specific effort on their part to do such deeds, but it was a lifestyle for them. It was such a lifestyle for them that there was never a line drawn for them separating their everyday way of living from what is labeled as "outreach" or "mission work." These people on the right were constantly driven by the call to live righteously and promote justice before God and neighbor at all times and at all costs. These people to the right didn't seem to regard their own personal success and achievements as the sign that it was okay to come out of the trenches and give up the fight. Their work endured until the end—right up until the day of judgment when the king halted their work and divided the world.

Then the king addresses the people on his left. In very similar fashion, he ordered their fate and presented a compelling case against them. Their crime was that they failed to acknowledge and assist with the needs of *all* of their neighbors. For this group, the judgment was not because they had not done any of these things for their neighbors, but instead it was the fact that they made distinctions about who should be considered a neighbor. The king clearly points out that in both cases his concern was for the "least of these" without prejudice. The group on the left may have indeed given food and drink, welcomed some and clothed others, taken care of many and visited a few. In fact, they defended themselves by asking when there was ever a time that they saw *the king* (and anyone of noble standing and status, for that matter) in a desperate situation and not tended to his needs. They ask: "When did we see *you* hungry…and did not help *you?*" But the king stands in solidarity with "the least of these"—those not deemed neighbors—and claims them as equal in status with him. It was not the royal court that these people overlooked, but the least of these—the ones they passed by each and every day. The king's response quietly echoes the question: Who is my neighbor?

The King of the 1960s has much in common with this king of the Matthew passage in that he too asked the question: Who is my neighbor? In the quiet recesses of his soul, he examined the situation before him and realized that this civil rights fight was not one that simply meant the liberation of his own people, but instead it meant a liberation that affected all people. He recognized that blacks would not always be the least of these, and

that sometimes, depending on the circumstance, another group of people in another time and another space would also be the least of these.

It isn't specified in the text as to the makeup of the groups to the right and the left, but one could assume that neither the right nor the left was made up of one particular type of people. The ones on the right, affectionately called "the righteous," were not just the poor, oppressed, captive, persecuted, hungry, and naked. Nor were the righteous just made of up those who always gave to the needy. But the group on the right was made up of some of each—those who stood in solidarity with one another, working tirelessly for a just world. Those whose giving was not just out of what they had, but particularly those who gave out of what they couldn't afford to give. Those who sacrificed their own freedom and victories until *all* could rejoice together.

And likewise, the group on the left was not a population of those who had, but didn't give and didn't care. But this group on the left was also made up of those gave so they could be acknowledged or gave only to a select group. These were also people who started the fight for justice, but celebrated too early or gave up due to fear, doubt, and loss of hope. This group included some of the least of these who had made it through the desert and forgotten those they left behind.

Nobody knows the makeup of these groups mentioned in our text for sure. This makes us all ask the question: Who is my neighbor?

The example of Jesus is a call to work for all God's people. For Jesus, the other, the stranger, the marginalized, the destitute, the voiceless, the powerless, the nameless, and the faceless are all his neighbors. If then we are followers of Jesus Christ—they have to be ours too. ✢

THE AFRICAN AMERICAN PULPIT

FORTHCOMING IN THE AFRICAN AMERICAN PULPIT

SUBSCRIBE TODAY.
You don't want to miss an issue in 2007!
Visit www.TheAfricanAmericanPulpit.com or call 1-800-509-TAAP.

SPRING 2007 - TOP TRENDS IN THE AFRICAN AMERICAN CHURCH
This issue will list the top 25 issues that have had the greatest impact on the African American church in the past 20 years. These will include TRENDS IN: Clergy Compensation; the Use of Titles; The Rise of the New Bentley 20 (Wealth Among Today's Preachers); and much, much more. This issue will be a collector's issue for all who want to know where the church is now.

SUMMER 2007 - GENERAL ISSUE FEATURING SOME OF TODAY'S MOST DYNAMIC PREACHERS
TAAP will continue to provide wide-ranging sermon offerings across denominational and non-denominational lines. Expect new names, elders, and historic material. It is our aim to ensure that African American preaching is codified, celebrated, and presented in formats that are stimulating and serve as teaching tools.

FALL 2007 - STEWARDSHIP AND CHURCH GROWTH
This issue will offer modern approaches to stewardship and information on church growth by leading persons in the field and by pastors who have figured out how to grow a church.

Is your church dying? Is your church doing okay but you know it is not living up to its full potential? Are you confused by all of the things you see on television ministry broadcasts? Are you wondering how to stay true to the Bible, be prophetic, and yet grow your church? If you answered yes to any of these questions, this issue is for you!

THE 10th ANNIVERSARY OF THE AFRICAN AMERICAN PULPIT

Visit our website throughout the year to learn about gifts and other surprises!

WINTER 2007 - THE NEW REVIVALISTS (Issue to include a CD)
We know the standard names who have proudly held up the mantle of proclamation in the African American Church for the past 30 or 40 years. But who are the new names? What voices have come upon the scene in the past decade to provide new methods, new styles, and new ways of reaching congregations? What's out? What's in? This issue will give you the full run-down on today's revival scene and will include a dynamic CD.

Elijah Is US

CAESAR A. W. CLARK

1 Kings 19:4, KJV

But he [Elijah] himself went a day's journey into the wilderness, and came and sat down under a juniper tree: and he requested for himself that he might die; and said, It is enough; now, O LORD, take away my life; for I am not better than my fathers.

It is night in the desert of Arabia. A day's journey out on the billowy sea of sand ridges and stony hills lies a living man—alone upon the bare earth—under the shelter of a low scrawny tree. The scene is one of utter and melancholy solitude. If it were day, the distant shore of green fields and grazing flocks and human homes could be nowhere seen. And the aspect of loneliness and desolation is made more oppressive and painful by

Caesar A. W. Clark is pastor of Good Street Baptist Church in Dallas, Texas.

the presence of this weary, prostrate man in the midst of the arid and lifeless waste. The sentinel stars are all out in fiery armor on the battlements of heaven, and the clear air is tremulous with their cold twinkling light. The whole circuit of the horizon presents the same undulating sweep of bare earth and stony ridges, as monotonous and melancholy as the waste of waters seen from the deck of the ship in mid-ocean. There is no breeze, no sound of voice or footstep in the air. The desert is so silent that the weary wanderer can hear the beating of his own heart and the flow of the life-stream in his own brain. Haggard and weary and travel-worn, the unhappy fugitive has flung himself upon the ground in utter despair, wishing that he might sleep in that solitude and never wake again. Far from the homes of humanity and the gentle charities of domestic life, he would gladly give up his body to be covered by the drifting sands and his bones to be bleached by the parching winds of the desert. He had had enough of life with all its vain hopes and bitter disappointments.

The world is so given up to wrong and falsehood and misery that to him it is no longer worth living in. He would rather die in darkness and solitude than ever see the face or hear the voice of his fellow man again. It is a dreadful thing for the human heart to sink to such a depth of wretchedness and despair. But who ever studied the great problems of life with a reasoning mind and a sensitive heart? Who ever surveyed and sounded the great ocean of human guilt and misery, listening to its melancholy moan as it comes down from far distant ages and rolls around all the continents and islands of the earth and heaves its dark waves of living wretchedness upon the shores of eternity? Who ever stood face to face with these dark and dreaded realities without shrinking for a moment from a share in such a mysterious and awful thing as life?

To those who have little thought and less feeling, the order of things in this world and the prospect for that which is to come may seem all plain. But to a great, generous, deeply sensitive soul, there will come hours when one will cease to wonder at the words which affliction and darkness wrung from the lips of the patient patriarch of old: "Let the day perish wherein I was born!"[1] And who is this weary and broken-spirited person, and what shall I more say? For time fails me to tell of the noble deeds and heroic exploits of such stalwarts as the Nat Turners, the Fredrick Douglasses, the Crispus Attuckses, the Prince Halls, the Booker T. Washingtons, the M. L. Kings, the George Washington Carvers, the Harriet Tubmans, the Sojourner Truths, and the Mary McLeod Bethunes.

Fresh and fearless from the mountains of Gilead, Elijah remembered the history which Israel had forgotten: The deliverance from Egypt by a strong hand. The march through the waves of the divided sea. The guiding pillar of cloud and fire that went before and after the countless host. The bread from heaven that failed not for forty years. The mount of the law veiled in impenetrable darkness and girt with a coronet of fire. The allotment of Canaan to the conquering tribes. The pomp and solemnity of the tabernacle and temple worship. The oracular responses from the mercy seat. The brightness of God's glory shining in the holy place. Elijah knew them all.

Now, the priests of Baal had set up the worship of nature on every high place and under every green tree. The people had been taught that pagan gods ruled the elements of fire and water by their mystic spells. But Elijah still believed that the sun and the clouds and the hills and the valleys, the streams and the fountains were in the hands of Jehovah—as they were when Moses smote the rock in the wilderness and living waters gushed out; as they were when Joshua commanded and the sun was stayed from going down; as when Samuel prayed and the Lord sent thunder and rain in the time of harvest.

So, the inevitability of a confrontation looms on the horizon. The wicked sovereign and the deceived people must be brought to recognize the power and sovereignty of their father's God. For this purpose Elijah suddenly presents himself before Ahab. This awesome one who can chain the undulating clouds and imprison the gusting winds and make the heavens as brass—has locked up the treasure of the kingdom of nature. But God's prophet can afford to wait! Let Ahab and Jezebel try their gods! The priests of Baal are many! Elijah is one! If Baal can break the drought and bathe the crusty face of the earth with a drenching rain, let him! If he can clothe the field with verdure and bring forth the harvest in its season, let him! Because the shepherd finds that the brooks are getting lower among the hills. The ploughman is startled to see the earth dry in the bottom of his furrow. The vintner looks at his vines and turns to the sky with increasing anxiety each and every morning. One year passes and no rain! Two years pass and no rain! Three years pass and no rain!

The inexorable sky is covered day and night with a dry, dusty haze out of which no clouds form and no dew falls. The sun grows red and dim as it descends in the western sky. The brightest stars make only a faint blur of light here and there in the zenith, and the outline of the distant hills is lost in the lurid air. The parched earth is all burnt over as with fire. The once fruitful fields are like ashes from a furnace. The hot wind drains the moisture from the leaf and living flesh. And the mean, suffocating dust storm sweeps over

Remember, as long as God keeps us in this world, it is for a great and good purpose, and he will always give us something to do. We have never done enough so long as there remains anything to be done!

the land like a simoom of the desert. The grass withers on the hillsides and in the valleys. The harvest turns to stubble before it is half grown. The groves give no shade, and the trees of the forest stretch their skeleton arms in mute supplication to the pitiless sky. The weary and heartbroken shepherd leads his panting herd from valley to valley in search of water, and daily the bleating of the flocks grows fainter among the hills.

Then the famine enters the homes of humanity. The feeble and the friendless die first, and the living in their despair have neither heart nor strength to bury the dead. Weary travelers and haggard, hollow-eyed victims of famishing thirst and gnawing starvation are thrown together in a heartless delirium of death.

But worse than any physical famine is the famine of lost faith in God—the famine in truth—the famine in love—the famine in devotion to duty—the famine in caring. This was what the prophet most came to change.

It all ends. The contest on Carmel was a dazzling success and an unmistakable vindication of Jehovah's honor and of the prophet's faith, courage, patience, and proclamation. The terrible excitement and the exhausting toil of day being ended, the weary prophet lays down to rest. But next a messenger comes from the city and tells the triumphant prophet of the threat made by Jezebel against his life! The prophet rises like one terrified by a dream and not yet fully awake. The prophet runs! But could we be

mistaken? Is that Elijah, the stout-hearted saint? Is that the fearless and courageous one? Is that the hero of Carmel? Is this the man who just a short while ago put a king to shame and turned back the hearts of the people to Jehovah? Is that the prophet who called down fire from heaven and brought rain from the clouds? Is this the prophet who infuriated the pagan queen Jezebel in her own palace by rebuilding the altar of Jehovah in the capital of the kingdom?

It is he! Running! Running over the hills of Samaria and the mountains of Ephraim, up and down the stony paths of Bethel and Gibeon, along the valleys west of Jerusalem and Bethlehem, and then out upon the plain of Sharon and on to Beersheba. Running! He dares not stop to rest! Leaving his only attendant behind him without a guide or provisions for the way.

He starts out in the early morning upon the wasted and lifeless desert. All day long he toils over the broken hills and barren plains of yellow sand and bare earth. The dead uniformity of desolation stretches in every direction. No living thing moves upon the earth or flies in the hot glimmering air. Now and then a suffocating blast swept over the horrible wilderness, and the shining sand rises and whirls in waves and columns of fire. And still he presses silently on until the sun goes down and the stars come out in the sky. Then, finding a low, solitary bush of desert broom, he casts himself beneath it—weary, hungry, discouraged, frightened, and in complete despair!

"It is enough—now, O Lord, take away my life." Such is the reaction which not unfrequently follows the most heartwarming experience! How often have we seen it. Peter makes his boast and draws his sword against a multitude. Yet ere long he is frightened out of all faith and courage by the accusing finger of a maid! Paul is caught up to the third heaven in visions of glory and paradise. He heard words of wonderful and ineffable meaning such as cannot be spoken to ears of flesh and blood. But soon, so soon after that there was "sent unto him a thorn in the flesh—a message of Satan." The Christian in John Bunyan's *Pilgrim's Progress* lodged in the Palace Beautiful—slept in the chamber called Peace. In the morning he saw the Delectable Mountains and Immanuel's Land. He started on his journey. But he did not go far before fear grabbed him and made him wonder in his mind whether he should go back or whether he should press on.

Many of you here are young, gifted, faithful, influential, popular, successful! Your health is firm. Your mind is active. Your feelings are warm. Your imagination teems with glowing imagery. Your body never complains of exhaustion, work, or pain! You are full of hope! Your friends are many! But by and by your steps will begin to falter; your eyes will grow dim. The wheels of life will move heavily. The mind will lose something of its vivacity and invention. The voice, once clear as a harp when fanned by zephyr breezes, will not ring as clarion as it once did. You will not be able to catch the salient and soul-stirring forms of appeal as you once could!

No matter how large you loom now, by and by you will begin to lose the magnetic power of drawing people to you! Your friends will fall away from you, one by one, and others will not come to take their place. Invitations you now get will go to others!

People who now stop to say "Howdy" will pass you by! You will see others increase while you will decrease! You who are now in the prime of life, loved and admired by all, will find it hard to be only pitied and forsaken in infirmity and old age!

The closing years of life are darkened with despondency, and many times before we are called away, we shall say with Elijah—"It is enough." The despondency of Elijah was all the more heavy and bitter because it followed so close on the heels of success! If we live long enough, Elijah is us.

To be laid aside by age or sickness or diversion of public attention is hard to live with. But remember, as long as God keeps us in this world, it is for a great and good purpose, and he will always give us something to do. We have never done enough so long as there remains anything to be done!

God has work for the aged, the afflicted, the suffering, the disappointed, the helpless, and the poor. The greatest work ever done in this world was done by one who was called a man of sorrows and who had nowhere to lay his head! The greatest success ever gained in this world was called a failure at the time. And the greatest victory was thought by humanity to be a shameful defeat! Take courage, my brothers and sisters! When the prospects are dim—take courage! When the burden is heavy—take courage! When the work moves slow and temptations and conflicts are many and strong—take courage! When nights are dreary and days are gray—take courage! When there are fears within and fighting without—take courage! Keep toiling! Keep praying! Keep preaching! Keep testifying! It belongs only to God to say when it is enough! ✤

NOTE
1. Job 3:3, KJV.

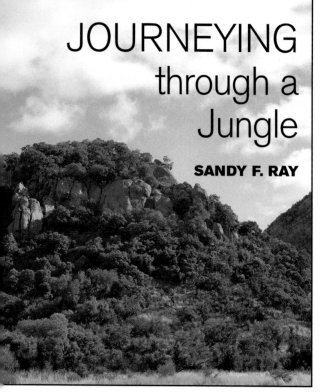

JOURNEYING through a Jungle

SANDY F. RAY

Matthew 3:1-3, KJV

In those days came John the Baptist, preaching in the wilderness of Judaea, And saying, Repent ye: for the kingdom of heaven is at hand. For this is he that was spoken of by the prophet Esaias, saying, The voice of one crying in the wilderness, Prepare ye the way of the Lord, make his paths straight.

The third chapter of Matthew's Gospel speaks concerning the appearance of a rather unique character who came on the scene with a flaming and frightening message. There was no specific date attached to his dramatic emergence. The record sets it in an indefinite period of "in those days."

It was evidently in that dismal period between the old and new dispensations—when accumulated corruption had silenced all voices of the Old Testament, when communication between heaven and earth had broken down, when all efforts to reach humanity in its fallen state had failed. That's when God planned a new thrust. God's love became reckless and extremely extravagant.

A strange character broke the silence of centuries with the announcement of the approach of the Messiah. When asked of his identity and his credentials, he replied: "I am the voice of one crying in the wilderness. My name is not as important as my message. The one who comes after me is mightier than I. My mission is to create a climate for him, to cut a small trail in this vast wilderness where his holy feet may tread."

John's wilderness tendency and thrust must have been shocking and embarrassing to his priestly father. His father was established in the community. He, no doubt, expected that his son would succeed him in the priesthood, but John had no interest in the formalities of the priesthood. He probably rebelled at being an altar boy. His father may have felt that he was losing his son. His father and mother may have agonized over their son's weird behavior. He was caught up in some far-out expectation of a coming Messiah.

The physical region in which John was preaching was not as much a wilderness as was the moral and spiritual jungle of society. There was exploitation and oppression of the poor from the Roman Empire. There was corruption and hypocrisy in the religious leadership. There was dire poverty and misery among the masses of the people. There was bold, brazen sin in the land in all of its ugly forms.

I submit that we also are journeying through a jungle at this period of our history. Through our various skills and technology, we have penetrated the physical jungles of this nation. We have highways, turnpikes, thruways, expressways, freeways, tunnels, bridges, boats, trucks, planes—forming various systems of

The late Sandy F. Ray (1898–1979) was pastor of Cornerstone Baptist Church in Brooklyn, New York. He is considered by many to be the Prince of Preachers. This sermon is reprinted from Journeying through a Jungle *by Sandy F. Ray (Nashville, TN: Broadman Press, 1979).*

transportation across the nation and around the world. But morally and spiritually we are journeying through a jungle.

The fact that we are journeying through a jungle is too obvious for argument. One only has to glance about to see this frightening forest which engulfs our society. Pickets, protests, demonstrations, strikes, riots in public schools, colleges, universities, factories, farms, hospitals, homes, and on municipal, state, and national levels. Wherever people live and labor, there is unrest and discontent.

The jungle has shifted from the forest to the front office. The jungle is no longer crude, primitive, stupid, simple, and rude. The jungle has become sophisticated, clever, and suave. The beast of prey is not hiding in a dark dungeon to pounce upon its victim. He is bold, brazen, and daring. This jungle is created by human behavior. Certain evil attitudes are allowed to grow unnoticed and unchecked until they form a forest where death-dealing beasts of prey hide.

The modern jungle is fashionable and fabulous. It is extremely attractive with glaring lights and fascinating entertainment. The jungle is often financed by millions of dollars and protected by bribery. Pimps and prostitutes walk our streets daringly and defiantly without shame or fear. Narcotics has become a most unholy and unhealthy industry. It is crippling and slaying the youth of the nation, physically, morally, and spiritually. The captains who control the jungle oppress the poor, underprivileged, underpaid, exploited, ghettorized, and untrained.

THERE IS AN OASIS IN THE JUNGLE

In their wilderness pilgrimage, the people of Israel found hopeful and inspiring oasis in the desert. There were glorious spots to break their gloom. There was a word from God that penetrated the terrifying darkness of their journey.

The wandering in the wilderness was not wasted years. The spirits of the people grew rugged through the disciplining of the wilderness. Jungles have instructive and disciplinary value. It is important for the people of God to understand the eloquence and rhetoric of the jungle. Many parents cripple their children by shielding them from the discipline of the jungle. They grow up with a timidity which leads to panic under pressure. Every child should have a jungle jolt to equip him or her for the hazards of life.

For several years it has been my privilege to speak to a large number of young ministers. Some of them are well trained with college and seminary degrees. Many of them are attempting to bypass the jungle. They would like a prestigious position dropped into their laps upon their graduation from seminary. They do not feel that they need the disciplining of the jungle. But the curriculum of the jungle is an essential part of ministerial training.

Moses, Elijah, and Jesus had the discipline of the desert. Moses on Mount Sinai, Elijah on Mount Carmel, and Jesus on Mount Calvary were products of their discipline in the deserts. They found oasis of hope and faith in the deserts. This may well be one of the reasons that God summoned them to the Mount of Transfiguration. They had undergone common jungle experiences before their final experience.

THERE ARE DANGERS
IN THE JUNGLE

Many animals in this jungle are clever and sophisticated, but extremely vicious and violent. Our society is full of hustlers, hippies, harlots, and hoodlums, pimps, punks, and prostitutes, cranks, crooks, clowns, and con artists, thrillers and killers, the lewd and the shrewd, and every conceivable brand of animal.

There is also the danger of getting caught in the brush and briars of the jungle and losing our trail toward the Promised Land. We can never know the number of well-meaning people in the world who are hung up in some thicket in this vast jungle. Many people with talent, gifts, promise, and potential are hopelessly bound by jungle briars. The mission of the Christian gospel is to break through the brush and briars and rescue captured souls.

Then there is the danger of becoming satisfied and contented with jungle life. The children of Israel had to be prodded ever so often and reminded that "This is not your rest." You must not accept the wilderness as your permanent home. We must enjoy the oasis, but we must not pitch permanent camp there. Saints may shout at an oasis, but the Promised Land still lies before them. The Christian church should always be an oasis in the jungle. It should be a haven for tired, wounded, footsore travelers. The most dedicated saints grow tired along this journey. Abraham, Moses, Joshua, Elijah, David, Paul, and even our Lord grew tired. The jungle is the only route to the Promised Land. There is no alternate route. The jungle is a part of the journey.

Some years ago, I spoke in a small Mississippi town. The word went around that there was trouble at the bus station. I inquired if there were other means of transportation in the town. I was told that there were no planes or trains out of the town. Friends took me near the bus station, and I fearfully asked for a ticket to New York. I was determined to get home, and that bus was my only means of getting there.

The jungle is our only route to the Promised Land. There will be fears and frustrations, handicaps and horrors, but God speaks loud and clear as we journey through the jungle: "Be not afraid, I am with thee." The history of the Hebrews is an abiding testimony of the power of God to deliver the people of God.

Many young people are torn by conflicting views as to what route they should take to get out of this jungle. They are revolting against parents, teachers, government, church, the system, and all conventional institutions. Many of

them are finding new "gods" through which to struggle for survival. Many of them are finding what Ahab found, that their god is not listening or is not able to deliver.

The jungle is frightening, depressing, and frustrating, but faith, hope, and experience keep a high expectation of deliverance in people of God. We have seen happy souls emerge from the jungle. When Israel panicked at the sea, the multitude turned on Moses, criticizing him for leading them into what they thought was a death trap. The record says that Moses prayed to God for orders in the crisis. God advised him to "stand still" and watch the Lord act. God sent a strong wind that divided the water and allowed the Hebrew people to walk through on dry land.

Our Lord Christ entered this jungle on a redemptive mission. The animals of jealousy, envy, hatred, and arrogance made their attacks upon him. When he was near the end of the jungle, the pressures were so great that he talked to his father about another way out of this terrifying jungle. But if there is no other alternative, "Not my will, but thine be done." The cross and the resurrection testify to the triumph of Christ's pilgrimage through the jungle.

The journey through the jungle is still rough and rugged. Providence subjects every soul, be you saint or sinner, to this hazardous pilgrimage. Evil persons may panic, but believers have sustaining faith in God for their journey.

John was "a voice crying in the wilderness." His voice disturbed the wilderness. The wilderness today is now crying for a voice—a prophet's voice. It may well be that the voice for which the wilderness is crying may not come from any of our national or international capitals. That voice may emerge from a jungle saint who has heard the voice of the Almighty.

May we walk calmly, faithfully, and expectantly through the jungle, realizing that this is the only route to the Promised Land. ❖

Numbers 13:30, KJV

And Caleb stilled the people before Moses, and said, Let us go up at once, and possess it; for we are able to overcome it.

L ike many a great man in every age—little known and less talked about—so is the great and good Caleb of Old Testament times. His birth and parentage have but little to do with the purpose of this discourse. It is the object to bring forward from amid the vicissitudious and antiquated history of Israel this retiring figure, stalwart Jew, and dauntless warrior, for the encouragement, enlightenment and example of us who are living today.

Caleb was a companion of Joshua, a subject of Moses; he was of the tribe of Judah and was called a Kenezite. Not much is known of him until Israel came to Kadesh-Barnea. 'Twas at this place, the Israelites wanted some human assurance of the condition and health of Canaan. God had described it and told them of its value and promised it to them in Abraham's day. The knowledge of the land and God's promise of it were among the things that made up the Jewish code of education. It would seem, with this traditional and documentary evidence, for a great deal of it had been written, that no Israelite could have questioned the facts concerning what was contained in the catalogue of promises; yet the incredulity of the people furnished a necessity, it would seem, for sending twelve spies over into Canaan in order to obtain information con-

CALEB

CHARLES ALBERT TINDLEY

cerning the land and its people and the possibilities of inheriting it.

In the number of twelve spies sent by Moses, Caleb is highlighted in the affairs because of the opposition in his report of the land to that of ten others. (No mention is made of Joshua in this chapter.) Upon majority report the Israelites based their faith and accordingly returned to the wilderness where they wandered for forty years, or until they were all dead save the faithful two, Caleb and Joshua. It is our purpose to make mention of noteworthy characteristics in the life of ancient Caleb.

1. His Estimation of God's Power Lessened the Terror and Magnitude of Opposition. The ten spies measured the vastness of the plains, the heights of the hills, the depths of the vales. They meas-

---

The late Charles Albert Tindley (1851–1933) was pastor of Tindley Temple Methodist Episcopal Church

in Philadelphia for more than thirty years and the author of some of the most beloved songs of Christendom. This sermon is reprinted from Book of Sermons, *Charles Albert Tindley, self-published by Charles Albert Tindley, Philadelphia, PA, 1932.*

ured the size and counted the number of inhabitants and compared all of this with the twelve spies themselves, and the feebleness of the host beyond the Jordan. Looking at these oppositions they themselves grew smaller, while the former grew larger, until they were reduced to grasshoppers in size, and the Canaanites to giants. This rationalistic calculation dwarfed and frightened the Israelites into an immediate retreat and turned their hearts back to Egypt. It did so then, it will do so now. Whenever human strength and device are pitted against enemies and oppositions, there is bound to be a retreat, not of the enemies and oppositions, but of the poor mortal who is attempting to wage the war.

The ten spies counted on Israel; Caleb counted on God. Israel was doomed to fail; God could never fail. The New Testament from the Pauline Scriptures is the echo of Caleb's faith. Paul said, "I can do all things through Christ which strengthened me." Caleb said, "If God be with us, we are fully able." He did not minimize the hills and giants, nor the multitudes; but he did magnify the Lord.

2. The Daring Courage to Do the Biddings of the Lord. It takes no coward to do God's will. This is not from a worldly standpoint, however, otherwise we would have to take it back, for nothing seems more cowardly than holding your peace when insulted; refusing to retaliate offenses, doing good for evil, and giving not rail for rail; but in reality and in the higher and better light of real manhood and worth the premium is placed upon the ability to control self rather than to subdue and control others.

In the light of the life of Jesus Christ we are coming to the knowledge that the real enemy of all of our best good and happiness lurks within one's own bosom. What can others do to beguile and make one sinful if purity and righteousness dwell within? What can the world do to make one unhappy if the happiness of heaven is within? That foe is your own evil sinful self, that enemy is the sin within that is sure to keep you from all that is good and happy.

It takes more than human courage and bravery to turn against one's self, to ignore the pride and disrespect the dignity and disobey the wishes thereof. Ah, of all cowards, this is the meanest, the man who will submit to the death dealing traits of his own character, and resent the slightest offense from without. Again it takes bravery to go against social currents. What others say and do, what others hold as popular and becoming is most apt to sway the actions of those who belong to their society. Men mistrust their judgments and charge themselves with error when their associates are all on the other side. But Caleb knew the truth and had the boldness to take the stand in the presence of Moses and all Israel.

3. His Willingness to Stand Alone for the Right. If I were asked to name the individual to whom in my judgment belongs medals and honors for bravery and for daring deeds—deeds that are good and helpful to others, deeds that are immortal and are going to enrich the world, I would select those who have the hardihood and bravery to stand alone for the right. Nor would I select such public characters whose every word and deed are seized by newspaper reporters and published in the world. That sort of bravery is certainly commendable in public life, but the ethical quality is, to say the least, a mist of ambiguity. Everybody enjoys honor and esteem, especially from those who are of repute for goodness and right thinking. Individual ambitions for honors and promotion would most likely solicit the praise and good will of the strongest people. In view of this fact, a man high in municipal or governmental affairs may make some very overt and plausible declarations that have the ring of righteous bravery or daringness, for no other purpose, or at least using this as the highest purpose, namely, to get the good will of the people and become promoted.

Such a state has so much real selfishness in it, and such an ambition so little or real righteousness as to be compatible with the possibilities of the worst sinner in the land. Jesus exposed the Pharisee who prayed and gave alms for a similar purpose. These real hypocrites are as whited sepulchers, as outside-shows. Far be it from me to say or to pretend that all deeds of the kind done by persons high in social or political life are of the above class and nature; nay, for some are as pure and noble of soul as can be found elsewhere. The least ambiguity and probability of hypocrisy are to be expected, where compensation in the way of public applause or promotion cannot be expected.

The humble layman amid his untoward surroundings, unseen by the public eye and unknown to the country, whose good deeds are not likely to be mentioned and whose bad deeds are comparatively unknown, such a one with little or no social incentives and positive persuasions of his fellows, must find the reason for doing good out of the real goodness of his own soul, and strength for desisting must come from a nobility unexcited by political or social emoluments or the praise of his fellows; it must be the result of real fortitude inherent as is the strength of the post against resistance or a wall against pressure.

There are many mothers in the home whose names will never be found in the columns of a public journal, and whose fame will never be rehearsed in the ears of the audience, who will stand up for every known duty and principles of right in the little circle of her home and in the presence of her children. I would ask for her a medal for real bravery.

A waiter in a fashionable hotel, where wines and all kinds of liquors are served, surrounded by an atmosphere of libertinism if he refuses to drink and partake of the sins before his eyes, may be greater than a member of the President's Cabinet, who refuses because of the opinions and criticisms of the nation he serves. Unpolished shining is an indication of pure metal, while polished shining may present a more brilliant lustre.

4. Our Hero Comes Before Us Now Because of His Untiring Zeal of 85 Years. Years full of toil and hardships, of anxiety and perhaps abuses rest upon his shoulders, his hair must have been streaked with gray, the ruddy youthful hue must have given place to furrows of age, but he stands by the side of General Joshua as straight as an athlete. His eyes twinkle with the same sparkling life and daring courage that gazed defiantly upon the ten cowards whose report he challenged in the valley of Moab, near the banks of the Jordan more than forty years ago. His soldierly bearing is the pride of every Hebrew boy, while his kindness of disposition has made him the idol of all the tribes of Israel. Out of their tenderness for him the elders had planned to give him an easy site in Palestine, but the old warrior refused, and asked for a place that would call again for the use of his how, his spear, and his sword. His throbbing patriotic heart has grown into that Christian zeal which finds its expression in the song of all lands:

"Sure I must fight, if I would reign;
Increase my courage, Lord."

No easy place for Caleb, no straggler on the road, no ambush in battle; to the front is his ambition, in the thickest of the fight is his pride. His old heart beats for the hill beyond Hebron; he would put his foot upon the burying ground of Machpelah and protect the dust of his ancestry. The giant must go; Anak must quit the place, for old Caleb will not unstring his bow until the foes are conquered.

WINTER 2005–2006

Talking about the Black Church and Social Security Reform: An Interview with Marie Smith, AARP President

Some Things They Did Not Teach You in Seminary: Shepherds Will Bleed, So Develop a Team by Frank A. Thomas

Articles: What the Church Can Learn from African Spirituality by Michael Battle; Developing an Effective Community Economic Development Ministry by Norman G. Bullock; Spirituality and the Black Church: What Must We Do? by Gayraud S. Wilmore

A Salute to the Church of Christ (Holiness) U.S.A.: The History Corner: Bishop Charles Price Jones (1865–1949) by James Abbington Jr.; Sermons: The Child Born to Us by C. P. Jones; Go Out in the Power of the Spirit! by Emery Lindsay

Sermons: A Matter of Choice by Gennifer Brooks; Hitting the Floor and Exposing Jezebel by Juanita Bynum; Frustrated by Victor M. Davis; Hide Moses by J. Delano Ellis II; The Anointing by Tony Evans; Residue by Eugene L. Gibson Jr.; The Nature of Acceptable Worship by Clarence E. Moore; When Religion Gets Dangerous by Carlyle Fielding Stewart III; While We Slept by Larry D. Trotter; With Simeon's Spirit by Lisa M. Weaver

Sermons from Some of the "20 to Watch": B.Y.O.B. by Gene J. Lawson; The Deciding Vote by Yvette D. Massey

SPRING 2006–PREACHING THROUGH YOUR PAIN

Introducing Our New Advisory Board Members

The History Corner: Bishop Daniel Alexander Payne by Marvin A. McMickle

Articles: How I Preach through Storms by Sheron C. Patterson; Pastoral Reflections While Traveling through a Storm by Leon Perry III; What Do You Do When Your Name Is Caught Up in a Scandal? by Joe Samuel Ratliff; Embracing the Process by Darryl D. Sims

Sermons: These Seventeen Words by Tyrone Crider; Uncompromised Convictions by Floyd Flake; The Way Back from Shame by Donald Hilliard Jr.; Living through a Life Storm by Derrick J. Hughes; I'm Coming Out with Praise by Jessica Kendall Ingram; Unforgivable Blackness by Alvin O. Jackson; How to Defeat Discouragement by Claybon Lea Jr.; All Things Work Together for Good by Barbara J. Morgan; Sanity in the Sanctuary by E. Dewey Smith Jr.; If God Is Pleased by Frank A. Thomas; Avoiding Self-imposed Storms by Terry Thomas; Overcoming the Spirit of Heaviness by Walter Scott Thomas; A Life That Only Death Affords by Wayne G. Thompson

"20 to Watch" Sermon: Come Out, Come Out, Wherever You Are by Cheryl D. Moore

SUMMER 2006

Tributes: An Interview with William Augustus Jones by Frank A. Thomas; *TAAP* Salutes Coretta Scott King; A Tribute to Rosa Parks by LaDonna M. Sanders

Articles: How Black Preaching Can Embrace Multiculturalism by Alise D. Barrymore; Religious Reasoning in Democratic Politics by David Bullock; Preaching from the Lectionary by Philip B. Davis Sr.; How Will Our Preaching Be Remembered? by Renita J. Weems; What Should Be the Black Church's Response to Wal-Mart? by Reginald W. Williams Jr.

Sermons from the 2005 Women in Ministry Conference: It Don't Make Sense, but It Works by Vashti Murphy McKenzie; I Can Produce by Gina M. Stewart

Sermons: The Word Whose Time Has Come by Charles Edward Bradford; Makes Me Wanna Holla' by A. Louis Patterson III; When Faith Takes Flight by RoyEtta P. Quateka-Means; The Three R's of Financial Responsibility by Martha Simmons; Don't Give Up on God by Ralph Douglas West; The Marks of an Irresistible Church by F. Bruce Williams; The Perfect Storm by Romell Williams Jr.; God's Word and Our Salvation by Ramah E. Wright; Lord, I Don't Think I Want This Anymore! by Juliet F. Zacharias

"20 to Watch" Sermon: The Revolution Will Not Be Televised by Sean H. McMillan

FALL 2006

Tribute: In Honor of Medgar Evers by Gene C. Young

Articles: Teaching Black Preaching: Encounter and Re-encounter by Dale P. Andrews; A Dance Ministry in Your Church by Denita Hedgeman; An Invisible Calling: The Role of Black Women in the Civil Rights Movement by Karen Jackson-Weaver; Preaching Faith to Heal Them: W. W. Austin and the Origins of the North Sixth Street Church of God in Christ by Elton H. Weaver III

Seminarians' Sermons: First Place: Why Seek Ye the Living among the Dead? by Jacqueline Blue; Second Place: By Whose Authority Do You Preach? by Christopher M. Jones; Third Place: The Hope in His Holler by Malene S. Minor; Priceless by Reginald Bell Jr.; The Ministry of Liberation: A Call and Response by D. Darius Butler; Ending the Identity Crisis: Do You Know Him? by Lisa M. Goods; A Grave Danger Disciples Face by Taft Quincey Heatley; A Message from the Original Promise Keepers by Benita Lewis; The World Is a Ghetto by Sylvia Moseley; A Glimpse of Glory by Dexter U. Nutall; Don't Settle! by Kimberly C. Rogers; God Says So…So Why Don't We? by Heidi M. Stevens; Considerations on the Cross by Jason Lawrence Turner; Who Is My Neighbor? The Stranger in Our Midst by Monica L. Wedlock

Sermons of the Elders: Elijah Is Us by Caesar A. W. Clark; Journeying through a Jungle by Sandy F. Ray; Caleb by Charles Albert Tindley